Ohio State Buckeyes Football

By The Numbers

Ohio State Buckeyes Football

By The Numbers

Researched by Tom P. Rippey III

Tom P. Rippey III & Paul F. Wilson, Editors

Kick The Ball, Ltd

Lewis Center, Ohio

This book is dedicated to Zach Padovan. His passion for football and desire to run one more play is unmatched.

Zach, good luck your junior and senior year and keep raising the bar.

Ohio State Buckeyes Football: By The Numbers;
First Edition 2010

Published by
Kick The Ball, Ltd
8595 Columbus Pike, Suite 197
Lewis Center, OH 43035
www.ByTheNumberBook.com

Edited by: Tom P. Rippey III & Paul F. Wilson
Designed and Formatted by Paul F. Wilson
Researched by: Tom P. Rippey III

Copyright © 2010 by Kick The Ball, Ltd, Lewis Center, Ohio

ALL RIGHTS RESERVED. No part of this book may be reproduced or transmitted in any form whatsoever, electronic, or mechanical, including photocopying, recording, or by any informational storage or retrieval system without the expressed written, dated and signed permission from the copyright holder.

Trademarks and Copyrights: Kick The Ball, Ltd is not associated with any event, team, conference, or league mentioned in this book. All trademarks are the property of their respective owners. Kick The Ball, Ltd respects and honors the copyrights and trademarks of others. We use event, team, conference, or league names only as points of reference in our books. Names, statistics, and others facts obtained through public domain resources.

LIMIT OF LIABILITY/DISCLAIMER OF WARRANTY: THE RESEARCHER AND PUBLISHER HAVE USED GREAT CARE IN RESEARCHING AND WRITING THIS BOOK. HOWEVER, WE MAKE NO REPRESENTATION OR WARRANTIES AS TO THE COMPLETENESS OF ITS CONTENTS OR THEIR ACCURACY AND WE SPECIFICALLY DISCLAIM ANY IMPLIED WARRANTIES OF MERCHANTABILITY OR FITNESS FOR A PARTICULAR PURPOSE. WARRANTIES MAY NOT BE CREATED OR EXTENDED BY ANY SALES MATERIALS OR SALESPERSON OF THIS BOOK. NEITHER THE RESEARCHER NOR THE PUBLISHER SHALL BE LIABLE FOR ANY LOSS OF PROFIT OR ANY OTHER COMMERCIAL DAMAGES, INCLUDING BUT NOT LIMITED TO SPECIAL, INCIDENTAL, CONSEQUENTIAL, OR OTHER DAMAGES.

For information on ordering this book in bulk at reduced prices, please email us at pfwilson@bythenumberbook.com.

International Standard Book Number: 978-1-934372-88-3

Printed and Bound in the United States of America

10 9 8 7 6 5 4 3 2 1

Table of Contents

Numbers 1-25……...………………….………..……….. Page 1

Numbers 26-50... Page 26

Numbers 51-75....................….………………....…Page 51

Numbers 76-100…………...………..………......……….. Page 76

About Kick The Ball, Ltd *By The Numbers* Books

"By The Numbers" books, articles, magazine features, etc. come in many formats. Most are done in pure chronological order, some match numbers in logical strings or related natural progressions within a category, and still others follow no easily discernable pattern at all.

As you turn the pages of this book, you will notice that we have categorized the numbers based on either the **final or final two digits** of each number. For example, you would find the year 1901 on page 1. The year 1910 would therefore be found on page 10, and so on.

In researching and compiling this book we found that to maintain our desired structure of a 1-100 grouping, this methodology would be necessary. Categorizing numbers 1-100 allows the reader to more quickly reference any given number based on the last digit or two, and gives us the ability to organize the data in exactly 100 pages.

This book is not meant to be exhaustive. Each researcher is given latitude to include a limited number of items they feel are particular important or interesting for each number. Additionally, other supportive or background numbers may be included with the primary number being presented. We do this to add depth to the information you are presented.

You will also notice **Featured Figure** sections spread throughout the pages of this book. These special sections include random, but interesting, information on a number relating to a particular moment or performance in team history.

All information in this book is valid as of the end of the 2009 season.

Ohio State Buckeyes

FOOTBALL

Ohio State played its first game on May 3, 1890, a 20-14 Buckeye victory against Ohio Wesleyan.

Ohio State's first head coach was Alexander S. Lilley. He led the Buckeyes to a record of 3-5 (.375) during his tenure from 1890-91.

OSU has appeared once in the Cotton Bowl, a 28-12 win over 8th ranked Texas A&M in 1987, and the Orange Bowl, a 27-10 win over 12th ranked Colorado in 1977.

One Buckeye has won the Davey O'Brien Award (Troy Smith, 2006), Bronko Nagurski Award (James Laurinaitis, 2006), Biletnikoff Award (Terry Glenn, 1995), Rimington Award (LeCharles Bentley, 2001), Ray Guy Award (B.J. Sander, 2003), Lott Trophy (James Laurinaitis, 2008) and Lou Groza Award (Mike Nugent, 2004).

OSU players have been singing "Carmen Ohio" to fans following games since Jim Tressel began the tradition in 2001. Players sing to fans in the south stands at home games and to the OSU section in away games. The song was written by Fred Cornell in 1898.

Ohio State's first forward pass came in a game against Wooster in 1906 under new head coach A.E. Herrnstein. It was a 10-yard touchdown pass from quarterback Walter Barrington to end Harry Carr. The Buckeyes won 12-0

By The Numbers

Ohio State Buckeyes

FOOTBALL

Two Buckeyes have been awarded the Walter Camp Award (Eddie George, 1995; Troy Smith, 2006), Butkus Award (Andy Katzenmoyer, 1997; James Laurinaitis, 2007), and Thorpe Award (Antoine Winfield, 1998 and Malcolm Jenkins, 2008).

Two former OSU coaches are in the Pro Football Hall of Fame (Paul Brown and Sid Gillman).

Although many underclassmen have been awarded the Heisman Trophy, Archie Griffin remains college football's only two-time winner.

Craig Krenzel is the only Buckeye to have received two bowl game MVP Awards. He was named MVP of the 2003 and 2004 Fiesta Bowls.

Les Horvath (1944) and Troy Smith (2006) are the only two Big Ten quarterbacks to have won the Heisman Trophy.

Ohio State has two players inducted into the College Football Hall of Fame for multiple positions: Warren Amling was inducted in 1984 as a guard and defensive tackle and Les Horvath was inducted in 1969 as a quarterback and halfback.

Only two Buckeye players have had 300 or more rushing attempts in a single season: Keith Byars (336 in 1984) and Eddie George (328 in 1995).

By The Numbers

Ohio State Buckeyes

FOOTBALL

Chic Harley was Ohio State's first three-time consensus All-American (1916-17, 1919). The only other Buckeyes to be named three-time consensus All-American are Wes Fesler (1928-30) and James Laurinaitis (2006-08).

OSU has played in three BCS National Championship Games (2002, 2006, and 2007), more than any other school.

Three Buckeyes have been drafted No. 1 overall in the NFL Draft: LB Tom Cousineau in 1979 to Buffalo, DT Dan Wilkinson in 1994 to Cincinnati, and OT Orlando Pace in 1997 to St. Louis.

Ohio Stadium's official capacity of 102,329 makes it the third largest on-campus stadium in the United States. The two largest on-campus stadiums are Michigan Stadium and Beaver Stadium respectively.

Jim Tressel has been named Coach of the Year three times: in 1991 and 1994 while at Youngstown State and in 2002 at OSU.

OSU has appeared in the Sugar Bowl three times (1978, 1998, and 1999).

Terrelle Pryor has recorded three games with 100+ rushing yards in his career. He is one shy of tying the Buckeyes' record for most career games with 100 yards rushing by a quarterback, currently held by Cornelius Greene.

By The Numbers

Ohio State Buckeyes

FOOTBALL

Four Buckeyes have won the Outland Trophy: Jim Parker (1956), Jim Stillwagon (1970), John Hicks (1973), and Orlando Pace (1996).

Four Buckeyes have recorded 150 or more receptions in a career: David Boston (191), Cris Carter (168), Michael Jenkins (165), and Gary Williams (154).

The Buckeyes have been awarded four National Championships by the Associated Press (AP) (1942, 1954, 1968, and 2002).

Four Buckeyes have recorded 1,000 or more receiving yards in a single season: Cris Carter (1,127 yards in 1986), Terry Glenn (1,411 yards in 1995), David Boston (1,435 yards in 1998), and Michael Jenkins (1,076 yards in 2002).

A top-ranked Ohio State team has lost four times in a bowl game. The No. 1-ranked Buckeyes lost to No. 11 UCLA in the 1976 Rose Bowl, No. 3 Southern Cal in the 1980 Rose Bowl, No. 2 Florida in the 2006 BCS Championship Game, and No. 2 LSU in the 2007 BCS Championship Game.

OSU has suffered four consecutive bowl losses twice, in bowl games following the 1977-80 and 1989-92 seasons.

By The Numbers

Ohio State Buckeyes

FOOTBALL

The most rushing touchdowns in a single game by an OSU player are five. Pete Johnson accomplished this feat in 1974 against North Carolina and it was matched by Keith Byars in 1984 against Illinois.

Eddie George recorded five career games with 200 or more rushing yards. In comparison, Archie Griffin (2), Chris Wells (2) and Keith Byars (1) combined for five career games with 200+ rushing yards.

Archie Griffin received five major college football awards in his career (Heisman and Walter Camp in 1974; Heisman, Maxwell, and Walter Camp in 1975), the most by any OSU player.

Five Buckeyes have been named Rose Bowl MVP: Fred Morrison (1950), Dave Leggett (1955), Rex Kern (1969) Cornelius Greene (1974), and Joe Germaine (1997).

Five Buckeye players have been inducted into the Rose Bowl Hall of Fame: Archie Griffin (1990), Rex Kern (1991), Fred Morrison (1993), Pete Johnson (2007), and John Hicks (2009). Woody Hayes was inducted as a coach in 1989.

The Buckeyes have appeared in five Fiesta Bowls (1980, 1984, 2003, 2004, and 2008).

By The Numbers

Ohio State Buckeyes

○ ○ ○ ● ● ●

F
O
O
T
B
A
L
L

Six Lombardi Awards have been given to Ohio State players: Jim Stillwagon (1970), John Hicks (1973), Chris Spielman (1987), Orlando Pace (1995 and 1996), and A.J. Hawk (2005).

Six Buckeye players are in the Pro Football Hall of Fame (Lou Groza, Dante Lavelli, Jim Parker, Paul Warfield, Dick LeBeau, and Bill Willis).

OSU has had six head coaches last one season or less: Charles Hickey (1896), David Edwards (1897), Howard Jones (1910), Harry Vaughn (1911), John Richards (1912), and Paul Bixler (1946).

Six games is the longest winning streak for the Buckeyes in the series against Michigan (2004-09). The longest winning streak in the series is nine; the Wolverines won the first nine meetings (1901-08).

Six OSU head coaches have been inducted into the College Football Hall of Fame: Howard Jones (1951), John Wilce (1954), Francis Schmidt (1971), Woody Hayes (1983), Earl Bruce (2002), and John Cooper (2008).

Featured Figure
Archie Griffin is the only college football player to have ever started in four Rose Bowl games.

By The Numbers

Ohio State Buckeyes

FOOTBALL

- The Buckeyes have been crowned National Champions seven times (1942, 1954, 1957, 1961, 1968, 1970, and 2002).

- Seven Heisman trophies have been awarded to Ohio State players: Les Horvath (1944), Vic Janowicz (1950), Howard "Hopalong" Cassady (1955), Archie Griffin (1974 and 1975), Eddie George (1995), and Troy Smith (2006).

- Southern Cal is OSU's most common opponent in the Rose Bowl. The two teams have met a total of seven times, most recently in 1985. The Buckeyes are 3-4 against the Trojans in "The Granddaddy of Them All."

In 2007, Zips linebacker Brion Stokes tackled Chris "Beanie" Wells in the end zone to give Akron a 2-0 lead in the first quarter. This was the last time OSU gave up a safety. The Buckeyes won the game 20-2.

Ohio State has started the season ranked No. 1 in the Associated Press poll seven times: 1942, 1958, 1969, 1970, 1980, 1998, and 2006.

The Buckeyes recorded seven touchdown passes against Pittsburgh in 1995, a single-game OSU record. Five of those touchdown passes were thrown by Bobby Hoying, one by Stanley Jackson, and one by Bobby's brother, Tommy Hoying. Ohio State won the game 54-14.

By The Numbers

Ohio State Buckeyes

F
O
O
T
B
A
L
L

OSU has played in eight BCS bowl games, most recently in the 2010 Rose Bowl. Ohio State is 5-3 all-time in BCS bowl games.

The last time OSU failed to score a touchdown was against Southern Cal in 2008. The Buckeyes lost 3-35 to the Trojans. Ohio State lost the yardage battle (207-348) and turnover battle (3-1). However, time of possession was in OSU's favor by more than four minutes. This is partly because three of Southern Cal's four offensive touchdown drives were 65 yards or less. Add to that a 48-yard interception returned for a touchdown right before halftime and what started as a good night with OSU going up 3-0, ended in a long trip back to Ohio.

In 2008, OSU became the fifth major college football program to post 800 all-time wins with a 25-14 victory over Ohio on Sept. 6. The Buckeyes' all-time record is 819-308-53, for a .717 winning percentage.

Eight times Ohio State has played back-to-back games against teams ranked in the top five. The Buckeyes won both games two times (1968 and 1996); won one game and lost one game three times (1972, 1974, and 2006); tied one game and won one game once (1949); and lost both games twice (1977 and 1997) for a combined record of 8-7-1 (.531) in those matchups. OSU's record is 5-3 in these games when entering the matchup with the better ranking.

By The Numbers

Ohio State Buckeyes

F
O
O
T
B
A
L
L

Terry Glenn set OSU's single-game receiving yards record against Pittsburgh in 1995. He had nine receptions for 253 yards.

OSU has had nine undefeated seasons. Five seasons with no losses or ties (1916, 1944, 1954, 1968, and 2002) and four seasons with no losses and one tie (1899, 1917, 1961, and 1973).

The last time the Buckeyes shutout an opponent was on Oct. 24, 2009. OSU beat the Aggies of New Mexico State 45-0. This was the third shutout of the season for the Buckeyes.

Ohio State set an average per game attendance record at Ohio Stadium in 2009. OSU home games averaged 105,261 fans during the Big Ten Championship season that culminated with a Rose Bowl victory.

The largest crowd to attend an OSU game was against Southern Cal on Sept. 12, 2009. The announced attendance of 106,033 marked the first time Ohio Stadium attendance surpassed 106,000.

Featured Figure

Michael Wiley started his OSU career with three touchdowns on three touches against Rice in 1996. He scored on a 49-yard reverse and two touchdown receptions of 51 and 60 yards.

By The Numbers

Ohio State Buckeyes

FOOTBALL

Ten former Ohio State head coaches have been inducted into the College Football Hall of Fame.

Vic Janowicz kicked 10 extra points against Iowa in 1950, the only Buckeye to have accomplished this feat. The Buckeyes beat the Hawkeyes 83-21.

The longest Ohio State drought between bowl games lasted 10 years. The Buckeyes failed to make a bowl appearance from 1959-68.

Howard Jones led OSU to a 6-1-3 (.750) record in 1910, the best winning percentage of an Ohio State head coach that lasted one season or less. Jones later coached at Southern Cal, leading the Trojans to victories against the Buckeyes in 1937 and 1938.

Bleachers were added to Ohio State's former home at Ohio Field in 1910, increasing capacity to 10,000.

John Lumpkin recorded ten touchdown receptions during his career at Ohio State (1995-98), the most career touchdown receptions by any Buckeye tight end.

Featured Figure

Ohio State head coaches that lasted one season or less had combined record of 27-22-9, for a .543 winning percentage.

By The Numbers

Ohio State Buckeyes

F
O
O
T
B
A
L
L

John Cooper led the Buckeyes to a record of 111-43-4 (.715) from 1988-2000. He and Woody Hayes are the only coaches to have led OSU to greater than 100 wins.

Archie Griffin rushed for 100 or more yards 11 times in the 1973 and 1974 seasons. Only Eddie George has recorded more 100-yard games in a season. George gained 100+ rushing yards 12 times in 1995.

In 1995, Terry Glenn broke Cris Carter's record for most receiving yards in a season. Glenn recorded 1,411 receiving yards on 64 receptions. Carter held the record for nine seasons. He recorded 1,127 receiving yards on 69 catches in 1986.

Only 11 Buckeyes have caught five or more passes and averaged 25 yards per catch in a single game. Dane Sanzenbacher most recently joined the list when he had five receptions for 126 yards against Toledo in 2009 for an average of 25.2 yards per catch.

Featured Figure

Three players have led the Buckeyes in rushing and receiving yards in the same season. In 1984 Keith Byars led the team in receiving with 479 yards and 1,764 yards rushing, in 1977 Ron Springs led the team with 90 yards receiving and 1,166 yards rushing, and in 1954 Hopalong Cassady led the team with 137 yards receiving and 609 yards rushing.

Ohio State Buckeyes

12

FOOTBALL

Andy Katzenmoyer recorded 12 sacks his freshman year. He only recorded six sacks in his next two seasons combined.

Ohio State joined the Big Ten in 1912, then known as the Western Conference. The Buckeyes did not begin conference play in football until the 1913 season.

The Ohio State campus has hosted ESPN's *College GameDay* 12 times. The show began visiting college campuses in 1993. The most recent appearance at OSU's campus was when the Buckeyes played Southern Cal in 2009.

OSU's record for highest total offense against Michigan is 512 yards. The Buckeyes set this record in a 50-20 victory against the Wolverines in 1961.

Twelve Buckeyes have accumulated 2,500 or more career rushing yards. Chris "Beanie" Wells is the most recent player to join the list.

Ohio State players have rushed for 100 or more yards in a single game 412 times. There have been a total of 103 performances of 150 yards or more, 16 of 200 or more yards, two of 250 yards, and only one over 300 yards.

By The Numbers

Ohio State Buckeyes

○ ○ ○ • • •

F
O
O
T
B
A
L
L

Thirteen Buckeyes have recorded 100 or more career receptions. Ted Ginn, Jr. was the most recent to join the list after catching 135 passes from 2004-06.

Two Buckeyes passed for 100+ yards in the same game 13 times, most recently when Craig Krenzel passed for 221 yards and Scott McMullen for 108 yards against Michigan in 2003.

The tradition of senior tackle started in 1913 by OSU head coach John Wilce. It currently takes place during the last practice before the Michigan game. Ironically, 1913 was the first time in 14 seasons that the Wolverines did not appear on OSU's schedule.

In Ohio State's first year of conference play in 1913, John Wilce led the team to a 1-2 conference record. The Buckeyes' only win came against Northwestern (58-0), with losses to Indiana (6-7) and Wisconsin (0-12).

Ohio State has only finished the season with a losing record in the Big Ten 13 times: 1913, 1918, 1922-25, 1927, 1943, 1946, 1959, 1966, 1988, and 1999.

Featured Figure

Tom Cousineau is the only Buckeye to have recorded 15 or more solo tackles in a single game. He had 16 solo tackles against Southern Methodist in 1978.

By The Numbers

Ohio State Buckeyes

○ ○ ○ • • • ──────────── 14

FOOTBALL

OSU has appeared in 14 Rose Bowls (1921, 1950, 1955, 1958, 1969, 1971, 1973-76, 1980, 1985, 1997, and 2010). Ohio State is 7-7 all-time in "The Granddaddy of Them All."

Fourteen Buckeyes have gained greater than 1,500 career receiving yards. Brian Robiskie was the most recent to join the list after gaining 1,866 receiving yards from 2005-08. Michael Jenkins holds the record with 2,898 career receiving yards.

The Buckeyes had 14 players selected in the 2004 NFL Draft, a school record for a single draft.

Fourteen years is OSU's longest drought between conference championships. The Buckeyes failed to win a conference championship from 1921-34.

The Buckeyes have played on Thanksgiving Day 14 times, most recently against Michigan State in 1912. OSU is 7-6-1 on Thanksgiving Day and it was the last game of the season each time. Ohio State played Kenyon its first nine Thanksgiving Day games, compiling a record of 6-3 in those matchups.

By The Numbers

• • • ○ ○ ○

Ohio State Buckeyes

FOOTBALL

The Buckeyes have passed for 15 or more first downs in a game on 14 occasions, most recently against Michigan in 2005. The only one that took place prior to 1981 was in 1952 when OSU passed for 15 first downs against Pittsburgh.

In 1980, OSU started the season ranked No. 1 and finished the season ranked No. 15 in the final AP Poll, its worst ranking after starting the season at the top of the poll. Ohio State ended the season with a record of 9-3. The three losses were to 11th ranked UCLA, 10th ranked Michigan, and 10th ranked Penn State.

The fight song "Across the Field" was written in 1915 by team manager William Dougherty. The song was first performed during a game against Illinois on Oct. 16, 1915.

Ohio State players have been named Big Ten MVP by the *Chicago Tribune* 15 times. Troy Smith was the most recent recipient in 2006. Archie Griffin is the only Buckeye to have won the award twice (1973-74).

OSU's record for most consecutive bowl appearances is 15. The Buckeyes appeared in a post-season bowl game every year from 1972-1986. A 6-4-1 and fifth place finish in the Big Ten in 1987 did not bring a bowl invite.

The team record for most consecutive conference home wins is 15 (from Nov. 4, 1967 through Oct. 30, 1971). The conference home-win streak was broken by a 10-17 loss to Michigan State on Nov. 6, 1971.

By The Numbers

Ohio State Buckeyes

16

FOOTBALL

Ohio State players have recorded 10 or more receptions in a single game 16 times. The only players with multiple games are David Boston (5) and Santonio Holmes (2).

Chic Harley became OSU's first consensus All-American in 1916.

OSU won its first Big Ten title in 1916. The Buckeyes finished 4-0 in conference play, outscoring their Big Ten opponents 90-29 and non-conference opponents 168-0. The 7-0 finish marked the first undefeated and untied season for the Buckeyes.

The Buckeyes have had 16 players named consensus All-American multiple times. James Laurinaitis was the most recent multiple consensus All-American (2006-08).

John Wilce is the second longest tenured head coach in Buckeye history. He led the Buckeyes to a record of 78-33-9 (.688) during his 16 years at the helm from 1913-28.

The team record for consecutive conference road wins is 16 games (from Oct. 22, 2005 through Oct. 3, 2009). The streak was broken by a 13-31 loss to Purdue on Oct. 17, 2009.

By The Numbers

Ohio State Buckeyes

17

F
O
O
T
B
A
L
L

Terry Glenn recorded 17 touchdown receptions in 1995, a single-season record at Ohio State.

OSU played three overtimes against NC State in 2003 for a total game time of 4 hours and 17 minutes, the longest game in Ohio State history. This was the first overtime game in Ohio Stadium history. Buckeye safety Will Allen secured the victory by stopping Wolfpack running back T.A. McLendon on fourth and goal from the one-yard line. OSU won the game 44-38 after blowing a 17-point lead with eight minutes left in regulation.

Ohio State played two postseason games in 1917. The Buckeyes tied Auburn 0-0 in Alabama and beat Camp Sherman, a team from Chillicothe, Ohio, 28-0.

The Buckeyes allowed only six points all season in 1917, outscoring opponents 292-6. OSU finished 4-0 in conference play and won its second consecutive outright Big Ten Championship. Ohio State has won the Big Ten conference outright two consecutive years three times: 1916-17, 1954-55, and 2006-07.

During their careers, Bobby Hoying and Art Schlichter each recorded 17 consecutive games with 100 or more passing yards. Schlichter recorded his over the last five games of 1980 and the first 12 of 1981. Hoying recorded his over the last four games of 1994 and the first 13 of 1995. The next highest total is 14, held by Troy Smith.

By The Numbers

Ohio State Buckeyes

F
O
O
T
B
A
L
L

OSU has won 18 Big Ten Championships outright. The last one was in 2009.

Ohio State only scored 18 points in 1897, compared to 168 points scored by opponents. The Buckeyes shutout Ohio Medical 6-0 in the first game of the season, tied Otterbein 12-12, and was shutout the other seven games.

World War I and a national influenza outbreak took its toll on college football in 1918. Diminished rosters led to games being cancelled and to other scheduling difficulties. The Buckeyes only played six games, the fewest since 1891.

Michigan resumed play in Big Ten football in 1918. Ohio State and Michigan played each other for the first time in six years that season and have played annually every season since.

The AP Poll began in 1936. Ohio State first appeared in the poll at No. 18, the week before the season finale against Michigan. The funny thing is, the Buckeyes beat the Wolverines 21-0 and did not appear in the poll for the remainder of the season.

Eighteen OSU players have recorded at least one kickoff return for a touchdown in a season. However, only one has actually recorded more than one. Lenny Willis returned two kickoffs for touchdowns in 1974.

By The Numbers

Ohio State Buckeyes

○○○••• —————————————— ⊕19⊕

F
O
O
T
B
A
L
L

OSU has won 19 bowl games. The most recent bowl victory was a 26-17 win over the Oregon Ducks in the 2010 Rose Bowl. Ohio State is 19-22 all-time in bowl games.

The Ohio State fight song, "Buckeye Battle Cry", was written in 1919 by Ohio University graduate Frank Crumit. The song is played during the band's entrance onto the field and during Script Ohio.

The Buckeyes beat the Wolverines 13-3 in 1919, OSU's first win against Michigan after going 0-13-2 in previous meetings. Ohio State only managed to score in four of the first 15 meetings, being outscored 369-21. The Buckeyes were shutout the first five meetings and did not manage to score until 1904.

Nineteen Buckeyes have won the William V. Campbell Trophy, formerly the Vincent DePaul Draddy Award. It is a graduate work-based scholarship given to 13 seniors annually and is based on excellence in athletics and academics. Craig Krenzel is the most recent Buckeye to win the award, a recipient in 2003.

Featured Figure
The Buckeyes have played at the Cleveland Brown's home stadium five times: 1942-44, 1991, and 2009. The only loss of the five games was against No. 5 ranked Purdue in 1943. OSU has played in the home stadium of the Cincinnati Bengals once, beating the Cincinnati Bearcats 23-19 in 2002.

By The Numbers

•••○○○

Ohio State Buckeyes

FOOTBALL

Twenty Buckeyes have a career average of 15.0 or more yards per catch (min. 50 catches). Brian Hartline is the most recent player to join the list, averaging 15.9 yards per catch from 2006-08. Only one player on the list played his entire career before 1980. Robert Grimes played for the Buckeyes from 1950-52. He had 50 catches for 755 yards for a career-receiving average of 15.1 yards.

Only four Buckeye quarterbacks have thrown 20 or more touchdown passes in a single season: Todd Boeckman (25 in 2007), Joe Germaine (25 in 1998), Bobby Hoying (29 in 1995), and Troy Smith (31 in 2006).

Ohio State's longest Big Ten winning streak is 20 games, which is also a conference record. OSU won every conference game from Oct. 15, 2005, through Nov. 10, 2007. The streak was broken when the No. 1 ranked Buckeyes lost 21-28 to the unranked Fighting Illini of Illinois.

The Buckeyes beat Southern Cal 20-0 at Ohio Stadium in 1960, which was the same outcome as the previous time the Trojans visited Ohio Stadium in 1948.

Randy Gradishar finished his Buckeye career with 320 total tackles, 12th on the all-time list. Woody Hayes said Gradishar was the best linebacker he ever coached. Gradishar was inducted into the College Football Hall of Fame in 1998. He was a seven-time Pro Bowler during his 10 seasons with the Denver Broncos.

By The Numbers

Ohio State Buckeyes

FOOTBALL

The Buckeyes have had 21 receivers record 50 or more receptions in a single season. DeVier Posey was the most recent, after pulling in 60 passes for 828 yards in 2009.

The 1921 Rose Bowl was Ohio State's first appearance in a bowl game. The undefeated Buckeyes lost 0-28 to the undefeated National Champion Cal Bears.

Ohio State has had 21 head coaches all-time.

John Frank recorded 121 receptions as a tight end during his career (1980-83), the most of any Buckeye tight end. His 1,481 career receiving yards is also OSU's record among tight ends, the only player at this position to surpass 1,000 career receiving yards.

OSU finished 5-2 in 1921, outscoring opponents 110-14. One of the touchdowns allowed resulted in a 6-7 Ohio State loss to Oberlin, the last time the Buckeyes lost to an in-state opponent. The second touchdown allowed resulted in a 0-7 Buckeye loss to Illinois. It was Illinois' first conference win of the season and the first conference loss for Ohio State. This was also significant as it was the last game at Ohio Field.

Featured Figure
OSU football turned a modest profit after 1901, its 12th season of play. It was the third consecutive winning season, with coverage in local papers helping to improve attendance.

By The Numbers

Ohio State Buckeyes

○ ○ ○ • • •

F
O
O
T
B
A
L
L

Les Horvath's jersey number 22 was retired by OSU on Oct. 6, 2001.

Twenty-two Buckeye players have been inducted into the College Football Hall of Fame. Chris Spielman is the most recent inductee (2009).

Ohio Stadium opened in 1922 with a construction cost of $1.3 million and an original seating capacity of 66,210. Current seating capacity at the Horseshoe is 102,329. The first game at Ohio Stadium was against Ohio Wesleyan on Oct. 7, 1922. The Buckeyes beat the Battling Bishops 5-0. The dedication game was against Michigan on Oct. 21, the third game in the stadium. The Buckeyes lost 0-19. They went 2-3 their first season of play in Ohio Stadium.

Ohio State's longest consecutive winning streak without a tie is 22 games. The Buckeyes accomplished this feat twice: from Nov. 4, 1967, through Nov. 15, 1969, (broken by Michigan); and again from Aug. 24, 2002, through Sept. 27, 2003 (broken by Wisconsin).

Antoine Winfield had 22 career tackles for loss, three more than Tom Cousineau and only eight fewer than OSU great Chris Spielman. He is the first non-linebacker to record 200+ total career tackles. In 1997, Winfield became the first defensive player ever named team MVP and the first cornerback to ever lead an OSU team in tackles. Winfield has played 11 seasons in the NFL and is 25th on its all-time interceptions list.

By The Numbers

Ohio State Buckeyes

FOOTBALL

In 1923 Ohio State finished 0-3 in conference home games, the second consecutive season without a home conference win. This is the only time the Buckeyes have failed to win a conference game at home in two consecutive seasons. OSU finished in eighth place in the Big Ten in 1922 and 1923.

The 1923 season was one of shut out or be shut out. Of Ohio State's eight games, the Buckeyes shut out their opponents twice and were shut out by the opponent three times. Two of the other three games were within one score of being a shutout either way.

Featured Figure

Mike Nugent holds nearly all kicking records at Ohio State: most kicking points in a season (120 in 2002) and career (356 from 2001-04); extra-point percentage in a season (tied; 1.000 in 2003 and 2004); field goals made in a game (tied with five), season (25 in 2002), and career (72); field-goal percentage in a season (.893 in 2002) and career (.818); most field goals made from 50+ yards in a season (5 in 2004) and career (8); most field goals made from 40-49 yards in a season (10 in 2002) and career (21); consecutive field goals made (24) and in Ohio Stadium (17); and is tied for the longest field goal made in Ohio Stadium (55 yards). Nugent has a clear lead over the second place player in most of the above categories. In 2004, he was named team captain, team MVP, and became OSU's first winner of the Lou Groza Award.

By The Numbers

Ohio State Buckeyes

FOOTBALL

Eddie George recorded 24 rushing touchdowns in 1995, his senior season. That season, George had a rushing touchdown in every game except for one and scored a high of four rushing touchdowns against Iowa.

Archie Griffin had 924 career rushing attempts, 241 more than second place Eddie George. Griffin had 159 attempts his freshman year, 257 as a sophomore, 256 as a junior, and 262 as a senior.

The first Big Ten win for the Buckeyes at Ohio Stadium happened on Oct. 4, 1924. Ohio State beat Purdue 7-0 to open the season. OSU would not have back-to-back seasons with more than one Big Ten home win until the 1933-34 seasons.

Ohio State was 24-0 at home during Archie Griffin's career as a Buckeye from 1972-75.

Buckeye great Shawn Springs wore number 24 as a Buckeye and recorded 24 career pass break-ups. He was named Big Ten Defensive Player of the Year in 1996 even though he did not record a single interception all season. Springs held Arizona State wide receiver Keith Poole to just one catch during the 1997 Rose Bowl. In that game, Springs had five tackles and four pass break-ups. He has played 13 seasons in the NFL and has been to one Pro Bowl (1998).

By The Numbers

Ohio State Buckeyes

F
O
O
T
B
A
L
L

Pete Johnson recorded 25 rushing touchdowns in 1975, an Ohio State single-season record.

The tradition of the Illibuck Trophy, the trophy awarded to the winner of the Ohio State-Illinois game, began in 1925. Members of the junior honorary society Bucket and Dipper from Ohio State and Sachem from Illinois meet at halftime to pass the trophy to the winner of the previous year's matchup. OSU has an all-time record of 58-27-2 in the trophy series, for a .678 winning percentage.

OSU quarterbacks have completed 25 or more passes in a game nine times. Joe Germaine and Art Schlichter are tied at the top of the list with 31 completions in a game. Joe Germaine has three of the nine spots and Troy Smith has two spots. Schlichter, Kirk Herbstreit, Craig Krenzel, and John Borton each have one.

Featured Figure

The Skull Session, a pre-game band rehearsal/pep rally that takes place two hours before kickoff, was started in the 1930s by band director Eugene Weigel. The event was moved to St. John Arena in 1957 and is regularly attended by more than 10,000 fans. Since 2001, Jim Tressel and the OSU players walk through the arena on their way to the stadium, with Tressel and a select number of players briefly addressing the crowd.

By The Numbers

Ohio State Buckeyes

FOOTBALL

ESPN's *College GameDay* has filmed on-location at Ohio State 26 times, most recently against Oregon in the 2010 Rose Bowl.

In his last game as a Buckeye, Michael Jenkins moved ahead of David Boston to No. 1 on the list for career receiving yards. Even though he needed every game played to lead the category, Jenkins set the record with 26 fewer career receptions than Boston.

In 1926, an announced attendance of 90,411 fans packed Ohio Stadium to watch the OSU-Michigan game, more than 34,000 above official seating capacity. A true safety hazard, this marked the last time Ohio State sold standing room only tickets.

The Buckeyes gained 26 first downs against Oregon in the 2010 Rose Bowl, an OSU bowl game record. Terrelle Pryor also set OSU's individual record for total offense in a bowl game with 338 yards.

The record for most consecutive wins at Ohio Stadium is 26. OSU won every home game from Sept. 16, 1972, through Sept. 11, 1976.

Jeff Logan recorded 2,026 career rushing yards as a Buckeye. He averaged 5.81 yards per carry. Among Buckeyes who have recorded 2,000+ career rushing yards, Logan ranks third in average yards per carry behind Archie Griffin (6.05) and Calvin Murray (5.88).

By The Numbers

Ohio State Buckeyes

○○○•••

FOOTBALL

27

Eddie George wore jersey number 27. His number was retired by OSU on Nov. 10, 2001.

A wooden turtle replaced live turtles as the Illibuck Trophy in 1927. Since then, there have been a total of nine wooden turtles used.

The point differential between Ohio State and its opponents in the 2002 season was 227 points, an average of 16.2 points per game. Most fans remember the close calls. Against Cincinnati, Craig Krenzel scored the go-ahead touchdown with 3:44 remaining. With less than a minute left, the Bearcats dropped two passes in the end zone and a fourth-down pass was tipped and intercepted by Will Allen. The game-saving pass from Krenzel to Jenkins in the Purdue game is a favorite among fans. Trailing 3-6 with just over one minute left, Tressel opted for the win instead of a field goal to tie the game. On fourth and one from Purdue's 37-yard line, Krenzel hit Jenkins, giving OSU a 10-6 lead following the PAT. The perfect season was capped off with a win against Miami in the 2003 Fiesta Bowl. The Hurricanes had a first down at OSU's two-yard line, needing a touchdown to send the game into a third overtime. On fourth and one, Cie Grant stopped Ken Dorsey at the one-yard line, securing an OSU National Championship. Even though the Buckeyes had other close calls against Wisconsin, Penn State, and Michigan, the Buckeye defense suffocated offenses the entire season.

By The Numbers

•••○○○

Ohio State Buckeyes

F O O T B A L L

Woody Hayes coached the Buckeyes for 28 seasons (1951-78) and led OSU to a 238-72-10 record. This is the longest tenure of any Buckeye head coach.

Oliver Cline gained 229 yards rushing against Pittsburgh in 1945, setting Ohio State's single-game rushing record. Archie Griffin broke the record 28 years later when he gained 239 rushing yards against North Carolina in 1972. The record has since been broken and is currently held by Eddie George, who gained 314 rushing yards against Illinois in 1995.

When comparing BCS conferences, OSU's best all-time record is against members of the Big 12 with a record of 28-5-1, for a .838 winning percentage.

OSU's record for most consecutive regular-season wins is 28 (from Oct. 15, 2005 through Nov. 3, 2007). The streak was broken by Illinois on Nov. 10, 2007.

OSU won its first game against Michigan in Ohio Stadium on Oct. 20, 1928. The Buckeyes beat the Wolverines 19-7. OSU wouldn't post consecutive home wins against Michigan until the 1934 and 1936 seasons. The Ohio State-Michigan series record is 39-38-4 in OSU's favor since the 1928 season.

OSU beat Oberlin 128-0 in 1916, the Buckeye record for most points scored in a single game and largest margin of victory. OSU scored 19 TDs and kicked 14 extra points.

By The Numbers

Ohio State Buckeyes

○ ○ ○ • • •

F
O
O
T
B
A
L
L

Chris Spielman recorded 29 tackles against Michigan in 1986, an OSU single-game record. The Buckeyes lost 24-26 to the Wolverines that game.

The largest Buckeye defeat in a bowl game was by 29 points. OSU lost 6-35 to Alabama in the 1978 Sugar Bowl. Ohio State was outgained by 126 yards. Although the Buckeyes only lost two fumbles, they put the ball on the turf 10 times. The No. 2 Crimson Tide played a flawless game with no turnovers and only one penalty for five yards, compared to OSU's four penalties for 40 yards.

The Buckeyes played the Battling Bishops of Ohio Wesleyan 29 times from 1890 to 1932. These are the most games played against any non-conference opponent. Ohio State leads the all-time series 26-2-1. The teams met every season from 1907-26. The Buckeyes won each of the 20 matchups during that span, outscoring the Battling Bishops 518-39.

Featured Figure
Jim Tressel played quarterback at Baldwin Wallace College located in Berea, Ohio. Tressel lettered in football from 1971-74 and represented the Yellow Jackets on the Ohio Athletic All-Conference team his senior year. He played under his father, Lee Tressel, who coached at the school for 23 years. Lee Tressel was inducted into the College Football Hall of Fame in 1996 and the football field at Baldwin Wallace is named in his honor, Tressel Field.

By The Numbers

• • • ○ ○ ○

Ohio State Buckeyes

F O O T B A L L

Joe Germaine completed 16 of 28 passes for 330 yards against Michigan in 1998, the most passing yards ever by any Buckeye against the Wolverines.

The temperature was five degrees with 30 mph wind gusts for the 1950 OSU-Michigan game. More than 50,000 fans attended what is now known as the "Snow Bowl." Officials from the Big Ten and both universities decided to play the game as scheduled and the winner would get a trip to Pasadena. If the game was cancelled, OSU would have won the Big Ten and represented the conference in the Rose Bowl. Although the Wolverines only gained 27 yards, they recovered a blocked punt for a touchdown and scored a safety to win 9-3. OSU's only points came off a 27-yard field goal by Vic Janowicz, an exceptional feat considering there was virtually zero visibility.

Chris "Beanie" Wells is the last Buckeye to record greater than 1,500 all-purpose yards in a season. He recorded 1,630 yards in 2007.

Troy Smith started his first game as a Buckeye against Indiana on Oct. 23, 2004. He led the Buckeyes to a 30-7 victory, helping Ohio State avoid their second 0-4 start in Big Ten history (OSU started the 1922 Big Ten season with four losses). For the day, Smith completed 12 of 24 passes for 161 yards and two touchdowns. He also added 58 yards rushing on 11 attempts. Justin Zwick, who was injured in the previous game against Iowa, never regained the starting position from Smith.

By The Numbers

Ohio State Buckeyes

F
O
O
T
B
A
L
L

31

Archie Griffin rushed for 100 or more yards in 31 straight games, an OSU record.

Vic Janowicz wore jersey number 31. It was retired by OSU on Sept. 23, 2001. All-time, only five Ohio State players have worn number 31, the fewest for any number.

In 1989, the Buckeyes trailed the Minnesota Golden Gophers 0-31 late in the second quarter. OSU scored on a Carlos Snow touchdown run just before halftime and Greg Frey completed a pass for a two-point conversion, narrowing the Minnesota lead to 23 points. The Buckeyes trailed 26-37 with just over five minutes to go, scoring the go-ahead touchdown with less than a minute left. OSU won the game 41-37, the largest comeback in Buckeye football history.

The Buckeyes lost 31-34 to Michigan in 1988, the highest point total for OSU in a loss to the Wolverines. Ohio State rallied from a 0-20 point halftime score, scoring on five of six second half possessions. OSU took a 31-27 lead with 2:02 remaining after former walk-on Bill Matlock's 16-yard touchdown run. Michigan's John Kolesar returned the ensuing kickoff 59 yards. Two plays later, Kolesar received a 41-yard touchdown pass to put the Wolverines up with 1:37 remaining. Ohio State was marching on what seemed to be a promising OSU possession. Greg Fry led the team to Michigan's 39-yard line before throwing an interception with 25 seconds remaining.

By The Numbers

Ohio State Buckeyes

○ ○ ○ • • • ───────────────── ─(32)─

F
O
O
T
B
A
L
L

The University of Michigan marching band was actually the first to perform script Ohio. They performed a script of OHIO diagonally across the field at Ohio Stadium in 1932. The Ohio State marching band would not perform their version of Script Ohio until October 10, 1936. The University of Illinois also performed a script of Ohio at Ohio Stadium on Nov. 14, 1936, after it had already been performed that day by the Ohio State marching band.

The lowest attendance average in Ohio Stadium history was during the 1932 season. The Buckeyes finished 2-1-2 at home, averaging 22,743 fans.

Jack "The Assassin" Tatum wore number 32 during his career with the Buckeyes. He is remembered for his intimidating hits. Tatum was named National Defensive Player of the Year in 1970. He played 10 seasons in the NFL and was a three-time Pro Bowler as an Oakland Raider. In 2001 Jim Tressel began awarding defenders the "Jack Tatum Hit of the Week."

Featured Figure

Ohio State had 11 fumbles against Indiana, losing 7 of them, in 1934, both single-game OSU records. Astonishingly, the Buckeyes still beat the Hoosiers 33-0.

By The Numbers

Ohio State Buckeyes

FOOTBALL

Archie Griffin rushed for 100 or more yards 33 times in his career, an OSU record.

Longtime Ohio State assistant Ernie Godfrey coached the Buckeyes for 33 years from 1929-61. He was line coach at OSU for 19 years and coached 13 All-Americans. Godfrey also served time as a defensive backs coach, freshman coach, and spent time working with placekickers. He served under seven Ohio State head coaches. Godfrey played end and center for the Buckeyes from 1912-14. Prior to joining the OSU coaching staff, Godfrey was the head coach at Wittenberg. He led the Tigers to a 63-24-8 record (.705), including two undefeated seasons. He was inducted into the College Football Hall of Fame in 1972. The Columbus Chapter of the National Football Foundation bears his name.

Gomer Jones played for Ohio State from 1933-35. He was a consensus All-American center for the Buckeyes in 1935. At 5'8" and 210 pounds, Jones was team captain and MVP in 1935. The Buckeyes finished the season 7-1, with their only loss to an undefeated Notre Dame team. Jones was inducted into the College Football Hall of Fame in 1978 and said his fondest memory as a player was Ohio State's come from behind victory against Chicago in 1935.

Featured Figure

The Buckeyes have had 100 or more offensive attempts in a single game twice: 101 against TCU in 1937 and 101 against Illinois in 1969. The Buckeyes won both games.

By The Numbers

Ohio State Buckeyes

FOOTBALL

34

OSU has won 34 Big Ten Championships, most recently in 2009.

OSU quarterbacks completed a combined 34 of 48 passes for 390 yards against Indiana in 1998, a school record for completed passes in a single game. The Buckeyes went on to beat the Hoosiers 38-7.

In 1934 Buckeye Head Coach Francis Schmidt began the tradition of honoring players with a pendant of gold pants for beating Michigan. He mentioned that Michigan players, "…put their pants on one leg at a time just like everybody else." His Buckeye teams outscored the Wolverines 114-0 from 1934-37.

The Buckeye Grove, located south of Ohio Stadium, started in 1934. Trees are planted in the spring to honor every OSU football first-team All-American. More than 125 trees have been planted to honor players as far back as Boyd Cherry in 1914.

Another annual tradition that started in 1934 is the captain's breakfast. Ohio businessman Walter Jeffery believed previous team captains should be honored. The first breakfast was held at the Scioto Country Club.

By The Numbers

Ohio State Buckeyes

FOOTBALL

Ohio State recorded 35 first downs against Houston in 1994. The Buckeyes beat the Cougars 52-0. This was the last time the Buckeyes recorded 35 or more first downs in a game. The only other times they accomplished this feat were against Utah in 1986 (36 first downs) and Drake in 1935 (39 first downs).

The tradition of Ohio State facing Michigan in the last regular-season game didn't start until 1935. The Buckeyes faced Illinois in the last game from 1919-33. In its first four seasons of Big Ten play, OSU finished the regular season against Northwestern.

The Buckeyes and Fighting Irish first faced off in 1935. Trailing 0-13 at halftime, Notre Dame started its second string in the third quarter to wear down Ohio State. After reinserting the starters, the Fighting Irish scored early in the fourth quarter. The Fighting Irish scored again with less than two minutes remaining to narrow the deficit to one point (both PATs failed following the first two scores). Ohio State lost a fumble on the ensuing possession. Notre Dame's fourth-string quarterback, Jimmy McKenna, scored the go-ahead touchdown with less than 30 seconds remaining. OSU lost the game 13-18.

The Buckeyes beat the Drake Bulldogs 85-7 at Ohio Stadium on Oct. 12, 1935. The 85 points scored by the Buckeyes is an Ohio Stadium record for points scored by any team in a single game.

By The Numbers

Ohio State Buckeyes

FOOTBALL

36

Eddie George gained 314 rushing yards on 36 carries against Illinois in 1995, setting the single game rushing record for OSU. This marks the only time an Ohio State running back surpassed the 300-yard mark. George also had four receptions for 32 yards. He scored two rushing touchdowns and one receiving touchdown.

OSU has had two players rush for 100 or more yards in the same game on 36 occasions, most recently in 2008 against Illinois (Chris Wells, 143 yards; Terrelle Pryor, 110 yards). Only one time has a player rushed for 200+ yards and another rushed for 100+ in the same game. This was accomplished when Loren White rushed for 209 yards and Donald Clark added 152 yards against Iowa in 1958.

Ohio State players have been named Academic All-American 36 times. Dave Foley is OSU's only three-time Academic All-American (1966-68). Five players have been named to the list twice: Brian Baschnagel (1974-75), John Frank (1982-83), Mike Lanese (1984-85), Greg Bellisari (1995-96), and Brian Robiskie (2007-08).

By The Numbers

Ohio State Buckeyes

FOOTBALL

Maurice Clarett set Ohio State's single-season freshman rushing record in 2002 with 1,237 yards rushing off of 222 attempts. His highest single-game total for the season was 230 yards against Washington State, which still ranks No. 6 on OSU's list of top single-game rushing records. His rushing total for the season ranks No. 17 all-time.

OSU and Penn State met for the first time in 1912. It was a particularly rough game with players on both sides suffering serious injuries. Frustrated with the play of the Nittany Lions, first-year Buckeye head coach John Richards complained to the officials throughout the game. When Penn State took a 37-0 lead with five minutes left, Richards led his team off the field. Penn State could not leave the field prior to time expiring in order to receive the win. Upset with the way the game was conducted, fans heckled the players during their wait. At times, police had to hold back angry fans. Once the last tick came off the clock, the Penn State Nittany Lions were officially awarded a 1-0 victory by forfeit.

The Buckeyes scored 337 points in their first National Championship season of 1942, setting a single-season team scoring record. That record would not be broken until the 1969 team scored 383 points.

By The Numbers

Ohio State Buckeyes

○ ○ ○ • • •

(38)

FOOTBALL

Ohio State's largest margin of victory against Michigan came in 1935 when the Buckeyes shut out the Wolverines 38-0. It could have been worse for Michigan. Two OSU touchdowns were called back due to penalties.

Block "O" began in 1938 and is Ohio State's largest independent on-campus student organization. The group was founded by Chris Isaac following a visit to Southern Cal where he witnessed a large student cheering section at football games. The organization has over 2,000 ticket holders, with designated sections located in both the north and south ends of Ohio Stadium.

Featured Figure

Since 1970 only four players have led the Buckeyes in tackles for three seasons. Marcus Marek was the first to accomplish this feat from 1980-82. Steve Tovar led the team in tackles from 1990-92; A.J. Hawk led the team from 2003-05; and James Laurinaitis led the team from 2006-08. Tom Cousineau and Damon Moore are the only players to lead OSU in tackles their sophomore and senior seasons, but not their junior season. David Adkins led the team in tackles in Cousineau's junior season and Antoine Winfield led the team in tackles for Moore's junior season.

By The Numbers

• • • ○ ○ ○

Ohio State Buckeyes

F
O
O
T
B
A
L
L

Chris "Beanie" Wells rushed for 222 yards and two touchdowns on 39 carries against Michigan in 2007, making him the only Buckeye to ever rush for over 200 yards against the Wolverines. The 39 carries and 222 rushing yards were also the most of any Buckeye for the season.

In 1939, the Buckeyes lost 14-21 to the Wolverines. Even so, Ohio State won the Big Ten Championship outright, the only time this has happened for OSU. The Buckeyes finished the season with a 5-1 record, just better than No. 2 Iowa at 4-1-1.

Ohio State beat Penn State 45-6 in 2000, the largest point differential in a loss for the Nittany Lions under Joe Paterno. This was OSU's fourth win in its five-win streak to open the season.

The Buckeyes trailed Penn State 3-7 to start the third quarter in the 2002 matchup. Ohio State's Chris Gamble intercepted a pass by Penn State's Zack Mills and returned it 39 yards for a touchdown with 13:07 remaining in the third quarter. It would be OSU's only touchdown for the day. Mike Nugent added another field goal to give the Buckeyes a 13-7 lead. The fourth quarter was scoreless and Ohio State remained undefeated, on its way to another National Championship. Ohio State outgained the Nittany Lions 253-179 yards.

Ohio State Buckeyes

40

FOOTBALL

Howard "Hopalong" Cassady wore jersey number 40. It was retired by OSU on Nov. 18, 2000. He held Ohio State's record for career all-purpose yards for 20 years until broken by Archie Griffin. Cassady's career total of 4,403 all-purpose yards still ranks fourth all-time, behind Griffin, Carlos Snow, and Tim Spencer. He averaged 122.3 all-purpose yards per game, which ranks third all-time behind Archie Griffin and Robert Smith.

Featured Figure

Chic Harley was the first of many outstanding players to put on a Buckeye uniform. Ohio State's record was 21-1-1 during his three seasons. He is OSU's first three-time consensus All-American [1916-17 and 1919]. Later he became a member of the first class inducted into the College Football Hall of Fame. Then in 1950 he and Jim Thorpe were named first-team halfbacks to the AP's All-Star college football team of the first half of the 20th Century. One of his biggest honors may be having his name forever associated with Ohio Stadium. Due to the overwhelming excitement he brought to Ohio State football, a new stadium was needed to accommodate all the fans. For this reason, many say plans were drawn up for the construction of Ohio Stadium, which is often referred to as "The House that Harley Built". Chic returned to Ohio Stadium in 1949 for a tribute in his honor. The marching band altered Script Ohio to Script Chic. This remains the only time the formation has ever been altered.

By The Numbers

Ohio State Buckeyes

○○○•••

FOOTBALL

Ohio high school football coaching sensation Paul Brown was named OSU's head coach in 1941. He coached the Buckeyes from 1941-43 and led them to a record of 18-8-1 (.685). He was sworn in as a Navy Lieutenant in 1944 and Carroll Widdoes was named interim head coach in Brown's absence. Brown returned to Ohio Stadium during the 1944 season as head coach of the No. 6 ranked Great Lakes Naval Training Center Bluejackets. The No. 4 ranked Buckeyes beat the Bluejackets 26-6. In early 1945, Brown was named head coach of the Cleveland Browns. He led the Browns from 1946-62 and later the Cincinnati Bengals from 1968-75. He was inducted into the Pro Football Hall of Fame in 1967.

Every Ohio State game since Nov. 18, 2006, has been nationally televised. That is 41 consecutive games.

Featured Figure

In 2006, Troy Smith became Ohio State's first quarterback to be named consensus All-American after leading the Buckeyes to an undefeated regular season. Six other Buckeye quarterbacks have been named to an All-American team (Harry Workman in 1923, Carl Cramer in 1931, Jim McDonald in 1937, Les Horvath in 1944, Rex Kern in 1969, and Art Schlichter in 1979), but none of them have been consensus All-American.

By The Numbers

•••○○○

Ohio State Buckeyes

F
O
O
T
B
A
L
L

42

Ohio State won its first National Championship, awarded by the AP Poll, in 1942. The Buckeyes moved up to third in the poll following the win against No. 4 Michigan. The next week, top ranked Boston College was upset by Holy Cross, No. 2 Georgia Tech lost to No. 5 Georgia, and OSU cruised to a 41-12 win over the Iowa Seahawks. When the final poll came out on Nov. 30, the Buckeyes received 93 more votes than No. 2 Georgia.

J.T. White was a player on the 1942 OSU National Championship team. Surprisingly, he was also a member of Michigan's 1947 National Championship team. Following his service in World War II, he decided to finish his college career at Michigan. White would later become an assistant coach at Penn State under Joe Paterno.

Pepper Johnson played in 42 games as a Buckeye. During his career he accumulated 379 total tackles, placing him third on the all-time tackle list in 1985 (currently sixth). He led the team in tackles in 1984 and 1985. Johnson played 12 seasons in the NFL and was a two-time Pro Bowler.

Featured Figure
A comment by Coach Jim Tressel during a post-game interview following the 2002 National Championship game gave chills to Buckeye fans nationwide. Tressel said, "We've always had The Best Damn Band in the Land, now we have The Best Damn Team in the Land!"

By The Numbers

Ohio State Buckeyes

○ ○ ○ • • •

43

F
O
O
T
B
A
L
L

Ohio State has an all-time record of 43-57-6 against the Michigan Wolverines, for a .434 winning percentage.

In 1943 the Buckeyes and Fighting Illini were called back onto the field 20 minutes after the apparent ending of the game. Officials discovered a penalty had been called against Illinois on the last play of the game. When they returned for one last play, OSU's Johnny Stungis kicked the only field goal of his career to win the game 29-26.

OSU outgained Cal 143 yards to 15 yards in the first half of the 1950 Rose Bowl, yet trailed 0-7 at halftime. Ohio State tied up the game 14-14 in the third quarter. With just over three minutes left, Cal mishandled a punt snap and the ball went out of bounds at the Bears' 13-yard line. OSU's Jimmy Hague kicked the winning field goal with less than two minutes remaining. And the Buckeyes won their first bowl game.

Featured Figure
The now famous kick, turn, and bow performed by the "i" dotter was an impulse reaction by sousaphone player Glen Johnson. During a performance in 1938, the drum major arrived at the top of the "i" too soon, so Johnson improvised to take up the additional time. The kick, turn, and bow instantly became a hit, becoming a part of the performance ever since. This new action also solidified the honor to future sousaphone players.

By The Numbers

• • • ○ ○ ○

Ohio State Buckeyes

○ ○ ○ • • •

F
O
O
T
B
A
L
L

44

Harold Henson gained 153 yards on 44 attempts against Northwestern in 1972. This is an OSU record for most rushing attempts in a single game. Only two other players have had 40 or more carries in a single game: Keith Byars had 40 against Michigan State in 1984 and John Brockington had 42 against Northwestern in 1970.

In 1944, Ohio State finished 9-0 under interim head coach Carroll Widdoes who was filling in for Paul Brown. OSU finished No. 2 in the AP Poll behind wartime favorite Army. The Buckeyes were invited to play in the Rose Bowl but the Big Ten faculty voted against the trip. The No.12 Tennessee Volunteers took OSU's spot, losing 0-25 to No. 7 Southern Cal.

The 1944 OSU-Michigan matchup marked the first time either team would win the outright Big Ten Championship with a victory. Ohio State won the game 18-14. On six other occasions the teams entered the matchup with an outright conference championship on the line. The Buckeyes won four of those games (1968, 1970, 1975, and 2006) while the Wolverines won two (1980 and 2003).

In Les Horvath's Heisman Trophy-winning season of 1944, he completed 14 of 32 passes for 344 yards and no touchdowns. Although Horvath was awarded the Heisman as a quarterback, he had a big impact running the ball. He had 141 carries for 807 rushing yards and 16 rushing touchdowns. Horvath did not play in 1943 and coach Carroll Widdoes had to convince him to suit up in 1944.

By The Numbers

• • • ○ ○ ○

Ohio State Buckeyes

FOOTBALL

Archie Griffin's jersey number 45 was retired by OSU on Sept. 30, 1999. Although not retired until 1999, Griffin's number was not issued to another player following the end of his Buckeye career. However, in 1996, Griffin himself agreed to allow Andy Katzenmoyer to wear #45. Katzenmoyer entered the NFL Draft following the 1998 season and #45 was soon retired.

Mike Vrabel leads all Buckeyes with 245 career sack yards (1993-96). Only four other players have 150 or more career sack yards: Eric Kumerow (163 yards from 1984-87), Matt Finkes (175 yards from 1993-96), Vernon Gholston (184 yards from 2004-07), and Jason Simmons (210 yards from 1990-93).

After leading the super sophomores to a National Championship in 1968, Rex Kern had his least productive season as a quarterback in 1970. Kern completed 45 of 98 passes for 470 yards with three touchdowns, all career lows. His low productivity as a passer did not limit Ohio State's success on the field. Kern's record as a starter was 27-2 from 1968-70.

Featured Figure
OSU trumpet player John Brungart dotted the "i" the first three times Script Ohio was performed. Currently the honor is bestowed to sousaphone players. Sousaphone dotters are required to have been a band member for four years in order to be eligible to dot the "i" in Script Ohio at OSU home games.

By The Numbers

Ohio State Buckeyes

FOOTBALL

46

Archie Griffin played in 46 games during his career with the Buckeyes. Thirty-three of those games he recorded 100+ rushing yards, 74 percent of total games played.

Even though Keith Byars played sparingly his senior year due to a foot injury, he finished his Buckeye career with 46 rushing touchdowns, second only to Pete Johnson's 56.

Robert Brugge had six receptions for 159 yards against Pittsburgh in 1946. He is the only player to average 25 or more receiving yards per catch in a game before 1979 (min. 5 receptions). He was also the first Buckeye to record 100 or more receiving yards in a single game.

Paul Bixler became head coach of the Buckeyes in 1946. He led Ohio State to a record of 4-3-2. Bixler resigned after the season to take a head coaching position at Colgate, citing too much pressure as a head coach for OSU. He was Ohio State's sixth and last head coach to last for one season or less.

B.J. Sander had a total of 46 career punts downed inside the 20. In 2003, he became OSU's first winner of the Ray Guy Award, which is given to the nation's best punter. That season, Sander had 39 of his 82 punts downed inside the 20, including seven in a game against Purdue. His perfect placement of kicks helped the Buckeyes win the field position game and he proved an excellent replacement for Andy Groom.

By The Numbers

Ohio State Buckeyes

FOOTBALL

Chic Harley wore jersey number 47 and was retired by OSU on Oct. 30, 2004. The last player to wear number 47 was Buckeye linebacker A.J. Hawk.

The only time Ohio State finished last place in the Big Ten was in 1947. The Buckeyes finished 1-4-1 in conference play with their only win coming against Northwestern. That win did not come easy. Trailing 0-6 with 50 seconds to go, the Buckeyes needed a penalty to negate a Wildcat interception. A Northwestern penalty after time expired gave the Buckeyes one more shot. OSU scored on a three-yard pass, tying the game 6-6. The Wildcats blocked the extra point, but were offside on the play. Ohio State kicker Emil Moldea connected on the re-kick to give the Buckeyes their one and only win of the season.

Art Schlichter completed 497 of 951 career passing attempts for 7,547 career passing yards from 1978-81, an OSU career record. Only seven other players have surpassed 5,000 career passing yards: Jim Karsatos (5,089), Mike Tomczak (5,569), Troy Smith (5,720), Steve Bellisari (5,878), Greg Frey (6,316), Joe Germaine (6,370), and Bobby Hoying (7,232).

Even though Big Ten and Pacific Coast (Pac-10) teams had previously met in the Rose Bowl, the 1947 game was the first under an agreement between the conferences to meet annually. Illinois beat UCLA 45-14 to give the Big Ten its first victory under the new agreement and second all-time.

By The Numbers

Ohio State Buckeyes

ooo•••

FOOTBALL

48

Gary Williams (1979-82) caught a pass in 48 consecutive games, an OSU record. He finished his career with 154 receptions for 2,792 yards and 16 touchdowns. Williams had eight career games with 100 or more yards receiving, placing him fourth on the all-time list behind David Boston, Michael Jenkins, and Cris Carter.

Mike Sensibaugh leads all Buckeyes in career interceptions and interception yards. He had 22 interceptions for 248 yards from 1968-70.

Featured Figure

Tom Tupa showed his versatility as a quarterback and punter for the Buckeyes from 1984-87. As a quarterback, Tupa accumulated 2,252 passing yards, good enough for 17th on Ohio State's list of career passing yard leaders. He ranks 11th on the OSU list for career completion percentage (.563). As a punter, Tupa was the first Buckeye to surpass 7,000 career punt yards. He finished with 9,564 punt yards, second on the list behind Brent Bartholomew (9,927). He is the only player to average 47 or more yards per punt in a season (47.0 in 1987 and 47.1 in 1984). His career punting average is 44.7, second only to Andy Groom's 45.0 average. Tupa played a total of 15 seasons in the NFL for six different teams, mostly as a backup quarterback the first five years and as the team punter the last ten years. In 1994, the NFL instituted the two-point conversion. And Tupa became the league's first player to successfully score a two-point conversion by running in a fake extra point attempt while playing for the Browns.

By The Numbers

•••ooo

Ohio State Buckeyes

F O O T B A L L

Ohio State's average home attendance has ranked in the top four in college football every year since 1949, holding the top spot 20 times during that period.

Archie Griffin had 22 carries for 149 yards and one touchdown in the 1974 Rose Bowl, setting OSU's record for rushing yards in a Rose Bowl. The Buckeyes beat the Trojans 42-21, a rematch of the previous year that ended with a 17-42 Buckeye loss. The six touchdowns scored in 1974 is a team record for most touchdowns in a bowl game and the six touchdowns allowed in 1973 is an OSU bowl game record for most touchdowns allowed.

The Buckeyes' first televised home game took place on Sept. 24, 1949. Ohio State beat the Missouri Tigers 35-34.

Former OSU head coach Earl Bruce joined the Buckeye football team as a freshman in 1949. Although Bruce was a standout high school player, he never lettered as a player at Ohio State.

Featured Figure
Four OSU linebackers have been named MVP of a bowl game: Rowland Tatum (1984 Fiesta Bowl), Larry Kolic (1985 Citrus Bowl), Chris Spielman (1987 Cotton Bowl), and Lorenzo Styles (1993 Holiday Bowl).

By The Numbers

Ohio State Buckeyes

○ ○ ○ • • •

FOOTBALL

The Ohio State University officially adopted the nickname Buckeyes for all athletic programs in 1950. The nickname has referred to Ohioans since William Harrison adopted the Buckeye tree as a campaign symbol in 1840.

The most points Ohio State has ever scored against Michigan is 50. The Buckeyes beat the Wolverines 50-20 in 1961 and 50-14 in 1968.

The only two players in Big Ten history to have a career passing efficiency of 150 or greater (min. 300 completions) are Troy Smith (157.1) and Joe Germaine (151.0).

Fred Morrison is Ohio State's only non-quarterback to win the Rose Bowl MVP. He was named MVP as a fullback after gaining 127 rushing yards on 24 carries in the 1950 Rose Bowl, leading the Buckeyes to a 17-14 win over Cal. This was Ohio State's first win in the Rose Bowl.

One of the best five minutes by a college football player took place at Ohio Stadium against Iowa in 1950. Vic Janowicz ran for a touchdown, passed for another, and returned a punt 61 yards for a third. He followed those scores by kicking all three extra points and sending two of the three ensuing kickoffs into the end zone. Janowicz was ultimately responsible for 46 of OSU's 83 points scored that day.

By The Numbers

• • • ○ ○ ○

Ohio State Buckeyes

FOOTBALL

Ohio State has played every team in the Pac-10 at least once. OSU has an overall record of 51-25-2 against Pac-10 members, with winning records against every team except for Southern Cal and Stanford.

Woody Hayes began his tenure as OSU head coach in 1951. He coached at Miami of Ohio prior to joining the Buckeyes. Miami became known as "The Cradle of Coaches," with names like Hayes, Bo Schembechler, Paul Brown and Ara Parseghian having an affiliation with the school.

Ohio State suffered its first loss of the 2000 season to the Minnesota Golden Gophers. The Gophers beat the Buckeyes 29-17, its first victory in Ohio Stadium in 51 years. This game marked the beginning of the end for John Cooper as Buckeye head coach. The Buckeyes ended the season with a loss to Michigan and to South Carolina in the Outback Bowl. Many thought that Minnesota head coach Glen Mason would be offered the head coaching position. Mason is an OSU alum who played under Woody Hayes and his team just upset the Buckeyes at Ohio Stadium. OSU athletic director Andy Geiger shocked college football when he announced the hiring of Youngstown State head coach Jim Tressel as Cooper's successor.

Featured Figure
Four Ohio State head coaches have won National Coach of the Year while at OSU: Carroll Widdoes (1944), Woody Hayes (1957), Earl Bruce (1979), and Jim Tressel (2002).

By The Numbers

Ohio State Buckeyes

FOOTBALL

Ohio State quarterback Art Schlichter attempted an OSU record 52 passes against Florida State in 1981. He completed 31 of them for 458 yards. However, the Seminoles had an equally successful day on offense. Both teams ended the day with 496 yards of total offense. The Buckeyes lost the game 27-36.

Fred Bruney intercepted three passes against Michigan in 1952, a Buckeye single-game record against the Wolverines.

John Borton passed for 312 yards against Washington St. in 1952. This is the only 300-yard passing game in Buckeye history prior to 1980. He recorded five touchdown passes for the game, which is also an OSU record he holds along with Bobby Hoying who accomplished this feat twice. Borton's passing efficiency for the game was 339.4, an OSU record. The only other Buckeye to record a single-game passing efficiency higher than 300 was Tony Curcillo. He had a passing efficiency of 326.6 against Iowa in 1951. The Buckeyes beat the Cougars 35-7.

Rich Spangler's 52-yard field goal against Southern Cal in the 1985 Rose Bowl is OSU's record for longest field goal in a bowl game. Even though the Buckeyes outgained the Trojans 403-261 yards, Spangler's three made field goals were the only Buckeye points for the first three quarters. Ohio State lost 17-20 to the top ranked Trojans.

By The Numbers

Ohio State Buckeyes

F O O T B A L L

Ohio State recorded its final tie, 53rd all-time, against Wisconsin in 1993 (14-14).

Troy Smith had a completion percentage of .653 in 2006, an OSU single-season record. He completed 203 of 311 attempts. The .600 mark has only been reached in seven other seasons: Jim Karsatos in 1985 (.612), Bobby Hoying in 1995 (.619), Stanley Jackson in 1997 (.600), Joe Germaine in 1997 (.614), Troy Smith in 2005 (.629), Todd Boeckman in 2007 (.639), and Terrelle Pryor in 2008 (.602).

Illinois gained 432 rushing yards against the Buckeyes in 1953, an Ohio State record for rushing yards allowed in a single game. OSU lost 20-41 to the Fighting Illini.

Featured Figure
A banner honoring Woody Hayes was unveiled during halftime of the Texas game on Sept. 10, 2005. It hangs on the east side of the stadium and is the only banner of a non-player displayed at Ohio Stadium.

By The Numbers

Ohio State Buckeyes

○ ○ ○ • • •

54

FOOTBALL

The Victory Bell, donated by the classes of 1943-45, first rung in 1954 to celebrate a 21-13 Buckeye victory over the Cal Bears. It weighs a whopping 2,420 pounds. Alpha Phi Omega fraternity members ring the bell following each OSU home win. The bell has been known to ring as long as 30 minutes following a victory against Michigan.

The Buckeyes finished 10-0 in 1954, culminating with a 20-7 Rose Bowl victory over Southern Cal. Their results included a win over No. 2 Wisconsin and victories over five other top-20 teams. This was OSU's first 10-win season and second National Championship. And it came at just the right time. The Buckeyes had won no more than six games in Woody Hayes' first three seasons and fans were anxious for a breakout season.

The Buckeyes recorded 54 shutouts under Coach John Wilce, 45 percent of games coached. Wilce's shutout total alone is more than the total number of wins by every Buckeye coach excluding Woody Hayes, Earl Bruce, John Cooper, and Jim Tressel. Those four coaches have combined to produce 66 shutouts in 657 games, or 10 percent of games coached.

Featured Figure

In 2001, Jim Tressel started a Wall of Fame in the Woody Hayes Athletic Center. It contains letters written by former OSU players and coaches on what it means to be a Buckeye.

By The Numbers

• • • ○ ○ ○

Ohio State Buckeyes

FOOTBALL

Woody Hayes voiced his displeasure with the Big Ten's decision to not offer athletic scholarships, something other conferences already started to adopt. With pressure growing from others within the conference, the Big Ten allowed a grant-in-aid program in 1955. This was the first year OSU instituted a form of an athletic scholarship.

A classic game between Ohio State and UCLA did not happen in the 1955 Rose Bowl. The undefeated Buckeyes were ranked No. 1 in the AP Poll and the undefeated Bruins were ranked No. 1 in the UPI Poll. Although the Bruins won the Pacific Coast Conference, a conference rule disallowed playing in the Rose Bowl two consecutive years. Since the Bruins faced Michigan in the Rose Bowl the previous year, they were not allowed to return to the game. Southern Cal represented the conference and the Buckeyes beat the Trojans 20-7. Ohio State quarterback Dave Leggett was named MVP of the game. OSU's Bill Booth ran the ball three times for 11 yards. Booth's father played for Pitt in the 1928 Rose Bowl and the two became the first father-son combo to ever play in the game.

In 1955, Paul Michael led the Buckeyes in receiving yards. He had four receptions for 50 yards. This is only one of three seasons since 1946 in which the leading receiver recorded fewer than 100 yards.

By The Numbers

Ohio State Buckeyes

FOOTBALL

Mike Nugent scored a total of 356 career points as a Buckeye from 2001-04 (140 extra points and 72 field goals), an OSU record.

The Detroit Lions drafted Howard "Hopalong" Cassady with the third pick overall in the 1956 NFL Draft. This is the highest draft position among OSU Heisman Trophy winners. Vic Janowicz was the lowest draft selection of any OSU Heisman winner. He was selected by the Washington Redskins in the 7th round of the 1952 NFL Draft.

The starting quarterback for the Buckeyes in 1956, Frank Elwood, attempted only 20 passes over nine games. Elwood completed seven of those passes for 86 yards. The leading passer for the season was halfback Don Clark who completed three of seven passes for 88 yards. Elwood led the team in passing in 1955 with 60 yards off of nine competitions and 23 attempts. Those are the only two seasons since 1944 that the leading passer had fewer than 200 yards.

The Buckeyes scored the first 56 points against 25th ranked Iowa in 1995. Eddie George recorded four rushing touchdowns and Bobby Hoying recorded one rushing and two passing touchdowns. The Hawkeyes scored just before halftime and came out re-energized for the second half. Although OSU's first string offense sat out the second half, the Hawkeyes limited the Buckeyes to fewer than 50 yards. OSU won 56-35 after the first half scoring frenzy.

By The Numbers

Ohio State Buckeyes

F
O
O
T
B
A
L
L

The first time 100,000-plus fans witnessed an OSU-Michigan game was in 1957. "The Big House" was packed with 101,001 fans who watched the Buckeyes beat the Wolverines 31-14.

Ohio State went 57 seasons without playing an in-state opponent. The Buckeyes beat Western Reserve (now Case Western Reserve) 76-0 in 1934. OSU would not play another opponent from the state of Ohio until 1992, when the Buckeyes beat the Bowling Green Falcons 17-6. Eddie George scored his first career rushing touchdown in this game. Ohio State has faced an in-state opponent annually since 1997.

Bobby Hoying passed for 57 touchdowns in his Buckeye career. As a starter, Hoying led OSU to a record of 30-7-1. Only three other Ohio State players have passed for 40 or more touchdowns during their career: Joe Germaine (56), Troy Smith (54), and Art Schlichter (50).

In 1957, the Football Writers of America and United Press International named the 8-1 Buckeyes National Champions over a 10-0 Auburn team, which received the Associated Press National Championship. Ohio State opened the season with a loss to Texas Christian. This is the only time OSU has opened with a loss and won the remainder of its games. The last three victories included wins over No. 5 Purdue, No. 19 Michigan, and a Rose Bowl victory over Oregon.

By The Numbers

Ohio State Buckeyes

○ ○ ○ • • • ⊕ 58

F
O
O
T
B
A
L
L

Ohio State beat Northwestern 58-0 on Nov. 13, 1913, to record its first conference win. The Buckeyes opened the season with a 58-0 win against Ohio Wesleyan. Even though the Buckeyes outscored opponents 154-27 in 1913, OSU finished 4-2-1 overall and 1-2 in conference play.

The NCAA added the two-point conversion in college football in 1958. Ohio State's first successful two-point conversion occurred following the first touchdown of the first game in 1958. Dick LeBeau received a pass from Frank Kremblas to put the Buckeyes up 8-0 against the SMU Mustangs.

Featured Figure
Ohio State has beaten a No. 1-ranked team four times. The unranked Buckeyes beat No. 1 Wisconsin 23-14 in 1952, No. 4 Buckeyes beat No. 1 Purdue 13-0 in 1968, No. 8 Buckeyes beat No. 1 Iowa 22-13 in 1985, and No. 2 Buckeyes beat No. 1 Miami 31-24 in the 2002 National Championship game.

By The Numbers

• • • ○ ○ ○

Ohio State Buckeyes

FOOTBALL

The Fighting Illini had 659 yards against the Buckeyes in 1980, the most yards ever allowed by OSU in a single game. In the game, Illinois completed 43 passes for 621 yards, both single-game OSU opponent records. Ohio State was outgained by 261 yards and recorded only 17 first downs to Illinois' 36. The difference was that the Buckeyes were plus six in turnover margin. And even though Illinois was able to move the ball through the air, the Buckeyes came away with a 49-42 victory.

Since OSU joined the Big Ten, the only time the Buckeyes and Wolverines have had a losing record in the same season was in 1959. Ohio State finished 3-5-1 (2-4-1 in conference play) and Michigan finished 4-5 (3-4 in conference play).

The last time the Buckeyes scored fewer than 100 points in a season was in 1959. Ohio State scored 83 points. OSU finished the season 3-5-1, the first of only two losing seasons under Woody Hayes. The other losing season happened in 1966 when the Buckeyes finished 4-5.

Featured Figure

Four defensive players have been inducted into the College Football Hall of Fame as a Buckeye: Warren Amling was inducted in 1984 as a defensive tackle, Randy Gradishar in 1998 as a linebacker, Jack Tatum in 2004 as a safety, and Chris Spielman in 2010 as a linebacker.

By The Numbers

Ohio State Buckeyes

FOOTBALL

Ohio State's 1995 matchup against Notre Dame was the first time the Fighting Irish visited Ohio Stadium in 60 years. There were 18 members of the 1935 Buckeye team recognized before the game. Unlike the previous matchup at Ohio Stadium in 1935, this time the Buckeyes trailed going into halftime (14-17). Also unlike the 1935 matchup, it would be the Buckeyes who took charge of the game in the second half as OSU built a 35-20 fourth-quarter lead. Notre Dame narrowed OSU's lead to nine points late in the fourth quarter. But Eddie George added another rushing touchdown and Josh Jackson added another field goal to give Ohio State a 45-26 lead to end the game. The 45 points scored by OSU was the most points ever allowed by a Notre Dame team under Lou Holtz.

Featured Figure

Ohio State coaches Earl Bruce and John Cooper both began their Buckeye coaching careers with a matchup against Syracuse. Bruce's 1979 team beat the Orange 31-8 and Cooper's team won 26-9 to open the 1988 season.

By The Numbers

Ohio State Buckeyes

F
O
O
T
B
A
L
L

Bob Ferguson led the Buckeyes in rushing in 1959 with 371 yards on 61 carries. This was the last time the leading rusher for OSU had fewer than 100 carries.

In 1961, the Buckeyes finished 8-0-1 overall, including 6-0 in conference play. Having won the Big Ten, Ohio State should have represented the conference in the Rose Bowl. However, there was no official contract in place between the Rose Bowl and the Big Ten due to a scandal that had taken place in the Pac-10. Therefore, school officials were given authorization to approve or disapprove the team's appearance in the bowl game. Ohio State faculty felt too much emphasis was being placed on the football team. In order to balance the importance of academics with athletics, they voted not to allow the football team to play in the Rose Bowl. A rally was organized to voice disapproval of the school's decision. Ironically the athletic department's own Woody Hayes would appear at the rally in firm support of the school's decision, telling those who arrived to return home. Ultimately he would provide not only the academic balance the faculty sought, but civic balance the community needed as well.

Ohio State was named National Champions in 1961 by the Football Writers Association of America. The Buckeyes leaped past Alabama after a 50-20 victory against Michigan. Alabama played two more games after OSU finished the regular season and was awarded the National Championship by the Associated Press.

By The Numbers

Ohio State Buckeyes

FOOTBALL

62

Ohio State started the 1962 season ranked No. 1 in the pre-season AP Poll. The Buckeyes finished 6-3 and ranked 13th. OSU outscored opponents 170-43 in its six wins and its three losses were by a combined 20 points. Fortunately, the season ended on a good note, with a 28-0 victory against the Wolverines.

Greg Frey recorded 2,062 passing yards in 1990, his third season with 2,000 or more passing yards. He is the only player to have accomplished this feat for three seasons. Frey also had 2,028 yards in 1988 and 2,132 in 1989. Only two other players have had two seasons with 2,000 or more passing yards: Craig Krenzel and Troy Smith.

Terrell Pryor led the Buckeyes in rushing in 2009 with 162 carries for 779 rushing yards. It was the first time in five seasons the Buckeyes failed to have a 1,000-yard rusher. The running back tandem of Brandon Saine (739 yards) and Dan Herron (600 yards) combined for 1,339 yards for the season.

Ohio State's 62-0 victory over Texas Christian in 1969 was the largest margin of victory for a Woody Hayes coached Buckeye team.

Jim Parker, one of the best offensive linemen to ever play for OSU, wore number 62. In 1956, he was named team MVP and became the first OSU player to win the Outland Trophy. Parker is enshrined in both the College Football and Pro Football Halls of Fame.

By The Numbers

Ohio State Buckeyes

F
O
O
T
B
A
L
L

David Boston had five receptions for 163 yards against Iowa in 1998 for a 32.6 per catch average, the highest single-game reception average of any Buckeye with five or more catches in a single game. He and Santonio Holmes (five catches for 150 yards against Michigan State in 2005) are the only players to average 30 or more receiving yards in a game.

OSU lost 14-63 to the top ranked Nittany Lions in 1994, the most points allowed by an Ohio State team since 1902. Penn State outgained the Buckeyes 572-214 yards.

Featured Figure

As Ohio State head coach from 1947-50, Wes Fesler led the Buckeyes to a record of 21-13-3 (.608). As a player for the Buckeyes, Fesler played end and was named consensus All-American in 1928-30. He was named Big Ten's football MVP in 1930. Also a star basketball player, Fesler captained the Ohio State basketball team in 1930 and became Ohio State's first consensus basketball All-American in 1931. Fesler was inducted into the College Football Hall of Fame in 1954.

Ohio State Buckeyes

FOOTBALL

Ohio State suffered its largest loss of the inaugural season against Wooster. The Buckeyes lost 0-64 to the Fighting Scots on Nov. 1, 1890. This game, the second in OSU history, was also the first-ever loss by the Buckeyes. The game was a home game for Ohio State, played just south of downtown Columbus at what was then Recreation Park. An Ohio historical marker was erected at the site in 2006 to commemorate the historic game.

Buckeye offensive lineman Jim Lachey wore number 64. Lachey only started four games for OSU prior to his senior season. His senior year, he anchored the offensive line that paved the way for Byars' record setting season. Lachey played 10 seasons in the NFL and was named All-Pro three times.

Featured Figure

Since 1944, only two Buckeyes have led the team in passing for two consecutive seasons with fewer than 500 passing yards each season. Frank Kremblas led the team in 1957 with 337 yards and again in 1958 with 281 yards. Joe Sparma led the team in 1961 with 341 yards and in 1962 with 288 yards.

By The Numbers

Ohio State Buckeyes

FOOTBALL

Brutus Buckeye first appeared in 1965. His name was chosen through a contest. A member of the cheerleading team, Brutus has appeared in various ESPN and Home Depot commercials and is seen regularly at every major OSU athletic event.

Buckeye fans have been singing along to "Hang on Sloopy" since 1965. The Ohio State marching band first played "Hang on Sloopy" against Illinois on Oct. 9, 1965. The song was number one on the charts the week before. Fan response was tepid the first time it was played by the band during a game. This may have been partially due to the heavy rain falling that day. However, fans went crazy when the song was played at the next game. It has been synonymous with Ohio State ever since.

Sixty-five Buckeyes have appeared in the Senior Bowl. The most OSU players from one season to appear in the game are six, from the 2004 roster. Bobby Hoying was named MVP in the 1996 game. He finished with 190 passing yards and two touchdowns.

Featured Figure
The Buckeyes' all-time record against BCS Conferences is: SEC, 7-11-2 (.400); ACC, 13-7 (.650); Pac-10, 51-25-2 (.667); Big East, 43-10-1 (.806); and Big 12, 28-5-1 (.838).

By The Numbers

Ohio State Buckeyes

FOOTBALL

Ohio State walk-on Billy Anders set the team record for receptions in a single season with 55 catches in 1966. He never even played football in high school. The record stood for 20 years. Cris Carter broke it in 1985 with 58 receptions.

OSU had its first back-to-back seasons with a 1,000-yard passer in 1965-66. Don Unverferth led the team with 1,061 yards in 1965 and Bill Long followed that up with 1,180 yards in 1966.

Mike Vrabel finished his career as Ohio State's all-time leader in tackles for loss. He recorded 66 tackles for loss from 1993-96. Only two other Buckeyes have recorded more than 50, Jason Simons (56.5) and Matt Finkes (59.0). Thirty-six of Vrabel's TFLs were quarterback sacks, a career list he also tops. Jason Simmons is second on the list for career sacks with 27.5. In conjunction with these two records, Vrabel is both the career leader in yards from tackles for loss (349 yards) and yards from quarterback sacks (245).

Featured Figure

In 1969, Jim Otis became OSU's first running back to record 1,000+ yards in a single season. He had 225 carries for 1,027 yards rushing. Since 1969 the Buckeyes have had a 1,000-yard rusher 25 of the past 41 seasons.

By The Numbers

Ohio State Buckeyes

FOOTBALL

Keith Byars had a memorable 67-yard touchdown run against Illinois in 1984, losing his shoe 35 yards before the end zone. Fans may recall Byars outrunning others on the field on his way to setting a then single-game rushing record with 274 yards. But what is often forgotten is how he led the team back from a 24-point deficit. His record-setting day also included five rushing touchdowns, tying Pete Johnson's single-game touchdown record. The Buckeyes eventually won the Big Ten and faced Southern Cal in the 1985 Rose Bowl.

In 1967 Billy Anders became the first Buckeye to surpass 100 career receptions. He ended his career with 108 receptions for 1,118 yards from 1965-67. Another player would not join him on the list of players with 100 or more career receptions until 1980. Doug Donley finished his career with 106 receptions (1977-80).

Ohio State lost 6-41 to No. 2 Purdue on Oct. 14, 1967, the largest point differential in defeat for a Woody Hayes-coached Buckeye team.

Featured Figure
Only two players have recorded five or more career games with 300+ total yards of offense: Troy Smith – five games from 2003-06; and Joe Germaine – six games from 1996-98.

By The Numbers

Ohio State Buckeyes

FOOTBALL

Woody Hayes began giving players Buckeye leaves in 1968 to reward team, unit, and individual accomplishments. For example, every player receives a leaf for each victory and one additional leaf for a Big Ten victory. Awarding Buckeye leaves was actually the idea of team manager Ernie Biggs. Nowadays, fans and players are accustomed to the expanding "leafy" area on players' helmets throughout the season.

The Buckeyes or Wolverines won the Big Ten every year from 1968-82, seven times for OSU and eight times for Michigan. From 1968-80, the teams scored exactly 176 points each in head-to-head games with a 6-6-1 record in those games. Also coincidental is the fact that both teams also had the same conference record from 1968-80.

OSU defensive lineman Jim Stillwagon wore number 68. He was a wall in the middle of the Ohio State defenses. In 1970 Stillwagon became the first player in college football history to have won the Outland Trophy and Lombardi Award in the same season. Even though the Green Bay Packers drafted Stillwagon in the 5th round of the 1971 NFL Draft, he opted to play for the Toronto Argonauts of the Canadian Football League. He played five seasons with the Argonauts and was a three-time CFL All-Star.

By The Numbers

Ohio State Buckeyes

FOOTBALL

With a 50-14 point lead against Michigan in 1968, the Buckeyes attempted a failed two-point conversion. After the game, Coach Woody Hayes responded to a question of why he went for two with, "Because I couldn't go for three." The following season, Michigan's new head coach, Bo Schembechler, made every player wear #50 in practice during Ohio State-Michigan week as a reminder of the agonizing loss. The 12th ranked Wolverines shocked the college football world in 1969 by beating the top ranked Buckeyes 24-12. This game marked the beginning of the "Ten-Year War" between Hayes and Schembechler. Michigan only won one Big Ten title in Hayes' first 18 years as OSU head coach. During the "Ten-Year War", the Wolverines won or shared eight Big Ten titles.

Jack Tatum became OSU's first consensus All-American defensive back in 1969. He was named consensus All-American again in 1970.

In the 1969 Rose Bowl, the top ranked Buckeyes faced the second ranked Southern Cal Trojans. After a scoreless first quarter, the Buckeyes spotted the Trojans 10 points. OSU tied the game 10-10 before halftime. Even though the Trojans' Heisman Trophy winner O.J. Simpson had a good day with 171 yards rushing, the Buckeyes opened a commanding 27-10 lead with 10 minutes left. Southern Cal scored with 45 seconds remaining, giving the Buckeyes a 27-16 win. Ohio State was awarded its third AP National Championship after finishing 10-0.

By The Numbers

Ohio State Buckeyes

FOOTBALL

Ohio State's highest winning percentage in a decade came in the 1970s when the team finished with a record of 91-20-3 (.811).

All-time, Ohio State has had 70 players selected in the first round of the NFL Draft, most recently DB Malcolm Jenkins and RB Chris "Beanie" Wells in 2009.

The Buckeyes have an all-time record of 70-0 when scoring 50 or more points. The last time OSU scored 50+ points in a game was against Northwestern on Sept. 22, 2007. Ohio State beat the Wildcats 58-7.

The senior class of 1970 featured six All-Americans, had a three-year record of 27-2, and was named National Champions by the AP in 1968 and National Football Foundation in 1970.

Joe Germaine is the most recent member of the 5,000+ career passing-yards club. He completed 439 of 741 passing attempts for 6,370 career passing yards from 1996-98.

In 1970, Woody Hayes placed a rug in the locker room that players had to cross to enter the practice field. It read: 1969 – Michigan 24, OSU 12; 1970 Michigan --, OSU --. Hayes had the rug made as a constant reminder of the upset the No. 1 ranked Buckeyes suffered to the Wolverines. It worked. Ohio State beat 4th ranked Michigan 20-9 in the 1970 matchup.

By The Numbers

Ohio State Buckeyes

FOOTBALL

71

The Buckeyes entered the 1971 Rose Bowl undefeated and ranked No. 2 in the country behind Texas. OSU would face off against the 12th ranked Stanford Cardinal, quarterbacked by Heisman Trophy winner Jim Plunkett. Ohio State outgained the Cardinal by 197 yards rushing, but the running play would bring demise. On fourth and one in the fourth quarter, Stanford stopped John Brockington just short of the first down. After regaining possession on downs, Plunkett led his team down the field for the go-ahead score and Stanford eventually won 27-17. The Buckeyes would have won another national title had they won this game. Texas lost to Notre Dame in the Cotton Bowl, which catapulted 3rd ranked Nebraska into the No. 1 spot.

Ohio State began playing 10 regular-season games in 1971, six years after other Big Ten schools.

During the OSU game against Northwestern on Nov. 13, 1971, former Buckeye head coach Francis Schmidt was honored posthumously for his induction into the College Football Hall of Fame. His plaque was presented to his widowed wife by former long-time Buckeye assistant coach Ernie Godfrey and Schmidt's former quarterback Tippy Dye. The Buckeyes lost 10-14 to the Wildcats, their first loss to Northwestern since 1963.

By The Numbers

Ohio State Buckeyes

FOOTBALL

The NCAA cleared freshman to play in 1972. This opened the door for a soon-to-be famous Ohio State freshman player that year, Archie Griffin.

Terrelle Pryor had 372 yards of total offense against Toledo in 2009. He had 12 rushes for 110 yards and one touchdown. He completed 17 of 28 passes for 262 yards and three touchdowns. Pryor joined a list of four other players to have recorded 350 or more yards of total offense in a game: Art Schlichter (412 yards against Florida State in 1981 and 353 yards against Purdue in 1978), Troy Smith (353 yards against Illinois in 2005, 386 yards against Michigan in 2004, and 408 against Notre Dame in 2005), Don Lamka (359 yards against Colorado in 1971), and Joe Germaine (388 yards against Penn State in 1997).

Harold Henson recorded 20 rushing touchdowns in 1972, the first OSU player with 20+ in a single season. Since then, only three other players have joined Henson on the list: Keith Byars (20 in 1983 and 22 in 1984), Eddie George (24 in 1995), and Pete Johnson (25 in 1975).

Featured Figure
The most consecutive losses the Buckeyes have suffered are five. This happened on two occasions: from Nov. 1, 1890, through Nov. 14, 1891, and again from Oct. 23, 1897, through Nov. 25, 1897.

By The Numbers

Ohio State Buckeyes

FOOTBALL

In 1973 Ohio State entered the Michigan game undefeated and ranked No.1. The Buckeyes came away with a 10-10 tie against the 4th ranked Wolverines. With a tie at the top of the Big Ten, the conference athletic directors voted on which team to send to Pasadena. The AD's chose Ohio State. Even though a national championship was out of reach, the Buckeyes beat the defending champion Southern Cal Trojans 42-21 in the 1974 Rose Bowl.

In 1973 three OSU players finished in the top six of Heisman balloting: John Hicks (#2), Archie Griffin (#5), and Randy Gradishar (#6). John Hicks is the only offensive tackle to have ever finished in the top two in Heisman voting. Penn State running back John Cappelletti won the trophy that year, beating Hicks by 533 votes.

Neal Colzie had eight punt returns for 170 yards against Michigan State in 1973, a Buckeye single-game yardage record. Only two other players have recorded 150 or more punt return yards in a game: Garcia Lane (161 yards against Purdue in 1983) and Tom Campana (166 yards against Michigan in 1971). Colzie also holds the record for punt return yards in a season, 40 returns for 679 yards in 1973. Only one other player has recorded 500 or more return yards in a season: Nate Clements had 39 returns for 513 yards in 2000.

By The Numbers

Ohio State Buckeyes

74

FOOTBALL

Tom Klaban kicked four field goals against Michigan in 1974, scoring all of Ohio State's points in the 12-10 victory against the Wolverines. This is the only time the Buckeyes have beaten the Wolverines without scoring a touchdown.

The Buckeyes began playing 11 regular-season games in 1974, three years after other teams in the Big Ten.

The Ohio State game against Minnesota in 1974 was the first road game to open the season for the Buckeyes in 63 years. The Buckeyes beat the Golden Gophers 34-19. The only other times the Buckeyes have opened the season at an opponent's home field was in 1890, 1892-94, and 1912. Ohio State won in 1890, lost the next three, and won in 1912.

In 1974 the Buckeyes entered the game against Michigan State undefeated and ranked No. 1 in the nation. In the eight games prior to this matchup, OSU outscored its opponents 360-75. However, the Buckeyes would struggle against the Spartans. Trailing 13-16 with less than 30 seconds remaining, Ohio State's Harold Henson was stopped short of the goal line. OSU hurried to get off the next play and a bobbled snap was picked up by OSU's Brian Baschnagel who ran it into the end zone. One official signaled touchdown while the other signaled time had expired. Undecided about the outcome, the official determination was not made until nearly 50 minutes had passed. Ultimately, the officials agreed time had expired and the Buckeyes suffered their first loss of the season.

By The Numbers

Ohio State Buckeyes

FOOTBALL

Ohio State has only played four teams 75 times or more: Wisconsin (75), Indiana (83), Illinois (96), and Michigan (106).

Pete Johnson had 1,059 yards and Archie Griffin had 1,450 yards in 1975, the only time two Buckeyes have recorded 1,000 or more rushing yards in the same season.

Lydell Ross was the season-leading rusher in 2004 with 475 rushing yards on 117 carries. This was the last time that OSU's season-leading rusher gained fewer than 500 yards.

Cornelius Greene was named Big Ten MVP in 1975. Although Archie Griffin won the Heisman that season and had won the conference MVP in his sophomore and junior years, Greene received the honor his senior year. Greene was the first black quarterback to start for the Buckeyes. He led the team in passing for three consecutive years, led the Buckeyes to three Rose Bowls, and was named MVP of the 1974 Rose Bowl. In 1973 Greene led the team with 12 rushing touchdowns. The star backfield of Griffin (7 TDs) and Pete Johnson (6 TDs) combined for only 13 that season.

Featured Figure

The 2009 senior class finished with 44 wins, the most of any senior class in OSU history. They played in a BCS bowl game all four years, including two BCS National Championship games. Their worst record was when they finished 10-3 in 2008.

By The Numbers

Ohio State Buckeyes

FOOTBALL

Jim Placenta led the Buckeyes in passing yards with 404 yards in 1976, the last time the season-leading passer had fewer than 1,000 yards. From 1944-75 OSU only had five seasons with a 1,000-plus-yard passer.

Vic Janowicz's personal best for most rushing yards in a single season was 376 in 1951. He had 250 carries for 802 rushing yards and six touchdowns during his Buckeye career. Janowicz was an excellent player on both sides of the ball. In OSU's wing formation, he ran, passed, and received the ball. An all-around athlete, he played two seasons with the Pittsburgh Pirates followed by two seasons with the Washington Redskins.

In 1976, Tom Skladany became the first specialist to be named team captain. He is also the first specialist to have earned a football scholarship with the Buckeyes. Skladany was named consensus All-American his junior and senior years. He ranks fifth on OSU's list for career punt yards (6,838) and career punting average (42.7). Skladany's punting average against Michigan in 1976, 52.3 yards, still ranks as the highest single-game average in OSU history.

Featured Figure
Art Schlichter is the only OSU quarterback to lead the team in passing yards for four years. He led the team in 1978 (1,250 yards), 1979 (1,816 yards), 1980 (1,930 yards), and 1981 (2,551 yards).

By The Numbers

Ohio State Buckeyes

FOOTBALL

Colorado was the first non-Pac-10 team the Buckeyes faced in a bowl game. The two teams met in the 1977 Orange Bowl. The Buffalos jumped out to a 10-0 lead. OSU quarterback Rod Gerald, who had missed the previous four games due to injury, came off the bench to lead the Buckeyes to a 27-10 victory. Ohio State only completed two passes during the game but outrushed the Buffalos 271 yards to 134.

Ohio State was co-Champions of the Big Ten in 1977, the sixth straight year as champion or co-champion of the league. This is a Big Ten record.

Featured Figure

In 1942 George Slusser became the first Ohio State player to pass for 100 or more yards in a single game. He recorded 120 yards against Pittsburgh in a 59-19 Buckeye win. Two games later, Paul Sarringhaus passed for 121 yards in a 21-7 victory against Michigan. The following week, Thomas James passed for 110 yards in a 41-12 victory against the Iowa Seahawks.

By The Numbers

Ohio State Buckeyes

FOOTBALL

Ohio State officially adopted the colors of Scarlet and Gray in 1878. A committee of three students met in 1878 to choose Ohio State's school colors. Orange and black were the original colors chosen. However, the committee changed its choice to scarlet and gray after discovering Princeton already had orange and black.

The last time OSU recorded more than 25 rushing first downs in a game was in 1978 when the team recorded 30 against Northwestern. The only other times the Buckeyes accomplished this feat was in 1977 (27 against Illinois) and 1974 (26 against Northwestern).

Woody's last win at Ohio Stadium was against Illinois on Nov. 11, 1978. The Buckeyes beat the Fighting Illini 45-7. Gary Moeller, a former OSU player and team captain for Hayes, was head coach of Illinois.

Bob Hope dotted the "i" of Script Ohio for Ohio State's homecoming game against Iowa in 1978. Raised in Cleveland, Hope and Woody Hayes were good friends.

Featured Figure
Only five OSU players have recorded 150 or more total tackles in a single season: Rowland Tatum (156 in 1983), David Adkins (172 in 1977), Marcus Marek (178 in 1982), Chris Spielman (156 in 1987 and 205 in 1986), and Tom Cousineau (211 in 1978).

By The Numbers

Ohio State Buckeyes

F O O T B A L L

Earl Bruce was named OSU head coach in 1979 and led the Buckeyes to an 11-0 regular-season record. His top ranked Buckeyes faced 3rd ranked Southern Cal in the Rose Bowl. Ohio State led by six points with just over five minutes remaining. The Trojans would have a final shot with a final possession beginning on their own 17-yard line. USC running back Charles White gained 70 yards on six carries during the last drive, evening up the score with a one-yard touchdown run. The Buckeyes perfect season was ruined following the extra point, losing 16-17 to the Trojans.

Calvin Murray's 86-yard reception from Art Schlichter against Washington State in 1979 is the longest reception in Buckeye history. Only five other times has an OSU quarterback and receiver hooked up for a pass play that went for 80 yards or more, most recently Santonio Holmes' 85-yard reception from Troy Smith against Notre Dame in the 2005 Fiesta Bowl.

Only 79 seconds remained when Ohio State began its final drive in the 1997 Rose Bowl. Jake "The Snake" Plummer, quarterback of the No. 2 rank Arizona State Sun Devils, led his team 95 yards down the field for the go-ahead touchdown with 1:40 remaining. Following the kickoff, the No. 4 ranked Buckeyes would begin a game-saving drive at their own 35-yard line. Two third-down conversions and an interference call later, OSU had the ball on ASU's 5-yard line. Joe Germaine hit a wide-open David Boston and he walked into the end zone, giving the Buckeyes their first Rose Bowl victory since 1974.

By The Numbers

Ohio State Buckeyes

FOOTBALL

Cedric Anderson had a career average of 21.3 yards per catch, and leads all Buckeyes in the category. He accomplished this with 80 receptions for 1,707 yards from 1980-83.

Bobby Hoying finished his Buckeye career with a .580 career completion percentage, the first OSU quarterback to surpass a percentage of .575. The only other Buckeyes to finish their career with a higher percentage are Joe Germaine (.592), Troy Smith (.627), and Todd Boeckman (.634).

Only six players have recorded rushes of 80 yards or more in Ohio State history: Joe Montgomery (80 yards against Iowa in 1998), Derek Combs (80 yards against Wisconsin in 2000), Tim Spencer (82 yards against Duke in 1981), Eddie George (87 yards against Minnesota in 1995), Morris Bradshaw (88 Yards against Wisconsin in 1971), and Gene Fekete (89 yards against Pittsburgh in 1942). Fekete is the only one out of the six that did not score.

By The Numbers

Ohio State Buckeyes

FOOTBALL

The 1981 Liberty Bowl was the only Ohio State bowl victory in which a Buckeye did not receive the MVP Award. Even though OSU beat Navy 31-28, Midshipman running back Eddie Meyers was named MVP after leading all players with 117 yards rushing off of 30 carries.

Craig Krenzel outrushed the entire Miami Hurricanes team in the 2002 National Championship game at the Fiesta Bowl. Krenzel had 19 carries for 81 rushing yards and two touchdowns. The leading rusher for Miami was Willis McGahee with 67 yards. As a team, the Hurricanes had a total of 65 rushing yards.

The 1981 matchup with Florida State produced a lot of OSU records. Gary Williams set records for single-game receptions with 13 catches and single-game receiving yards with 220 (both have since been broken). He became the first receiver to gain 200+ yards in a game (now joined by three others). Art Schlichter set various passing records: passing yards in a game (458), pass attempts (52), completions (31; tied with Joe Germaine), total offense (412; he still holds each record). And he is the only player to record 400+ yards in a game. Even though Schlichter had a record-breaking day, the 7th ranked Buckeyes lost the game 27-36.

By The Numbers

Ohio State Buckeyes

FOOTBALL

A BY THE NUMBERS

Cedric Anderson had 20 receptions for 552 yards in 1982, for an average of 27.6 yards per catch. Among those with at least 20 catches in a season, Anderson has the highest per-catch average of any Buckeye. Brian Hartline is second on the list behind Anderson in average yards per catch in a season. Hartline had 21 catches for 479 yards in 2008 for an average of 22.8 yards per catch.

Thirty points is the largest Buckeye margin of victory in a bowl game. Ohio State beat BYU 47-17 in the 1982 Holiday Bowl. OSU's 47-point total is the Buckeye record for most points scored in a bowl game. The Buckeyes racked up 345 rushing yards and two rushing touchdowns each for Tim Spencer and Jimmy Gayle. In the game, linebacker Marcus Marek recorded eight tackles to surpass Tom Cousineau's career tackle record. Marek finished his career with 572 tackles, three more than Cousineau.

Ohio State lost 0-6 to Wisconsin in 1982, the Buckeyes' first-ever loss to the Badgers in Ohio Stadium. This was the third loss of the season and the third in a row at home, only the second time this has happened at Ohio Stadium. OSU finished the season 9-3 and second in the Big Ten.

Only 5,482 fans showed up for Ohio State's matchup against Wilmington on Nov. 6, 1926, a single-game low for attendance at Ohio Stadium. This is surprising since the Buckeyes entered the game with a 5-0 record. Fans in attendance saw OSU go to 6-0 by beating the Quakers 13-7.

Ohio State Buckeyes

FOOTBALL

Ohio State was penalized 98 times for 883 yards in 2000, team records for number of times and yardage in a season. The Buckeyes were penalized 13 times for 136 yards against Fresno State that season, which is a single-game record for yards penalized.

Woody Hayes dotted the "i" of Script Ohio for Ohio State's game against Wisconsin in 1983.

Garcia Lane scored on two punt returns against Purdue in 1983, the only OSU player to have returned a punt for a score more than one time in a game. He ended up with 161 punt return yards for the day in Ohio State's 33-22 win against the Boilermakers.

Chris Spielman leads all Buckeyes with 283 career solo tackles. Spielman also had 105 solo tackles in 1986, which is also an OSU record for a single season. He played 10 seasons in the NFL and was a four-time Pro Bowler. He is the franchise-leading tackler for the Detroit Lions with 1,138 career tackles, 349 more than the second place player on the list, and holds the top three spots for most tackles in a season.

Featured Figure
OSU defensive lineman Heath Queen is the only player to letter with a last name that starts with a 'Q' (1998-00). The most common last name is Smith. Twenty-nine players were named Smith. The next most common is Miller with 14.

By The Numbers

Ohio State Buckeyes

FOOTBALL

Ohio State had 84 rushing attempts against Illinois in 1973, a school record. The Buckeyes beat the Fighting Illini 30-0. Illinois was held to only 74 yards of offense for the game.

In 1984, Keith Byars led the nation in rushing yards (1,655), all-purpose yards (2,284), and points scored (144).

Chris Spielman recorded 10 tackles after coming off the bench against Oregon in 1984. This game marked his college football debut.

Ohio State beat the Pittsburgh Panthers 28-23 in the 1984 Fiesta Bowl. Ohio State held a 14-7 lead entering the fourth quarter. The two teams combined for 30 points in the last fifteen minutes. Pitt took a one-point lead with 2:39 left to play. On the final drive, Thad Jemison received a pass from Mike Tomczak and scored with 39 seconds remaining. The Panthers were able to get to OSU's 24-yard line on the ensuing drive. But the game ended before the drive was over. Jemison tied a Fiesta Bowl record with eight receptions and was named game MVP for his performance.

Featured Figure
Many OSU single-game records that still stand today were set during the 1950 Snow Bowl against Michigan: most punts in a game (21), fewest total yards allowed (27), fewest yards allowed per attempt (0.6), fewest first downs allowed (0), punting yards (685), opponent punt attempts (24), opponent punting yards (723), and punts blocked (4).

By The Numbers

Ohio State Buckeyes

F
O
O
T
B
A
L
L

David Boston holds OSU's record for receptions in a single season. He caught 85 passes for 1,435 yards in 1998. He is also second with 73 catches for 970 yards in 1997.

Art Schlichter was responsible for 85 career touchdowns as a Buckeye from 1978-81, an OSU record.

Ohio State flanker Mike Lanese was named a Rhodes Scholar in 1985, the only Buckeye and most recent Big Ten football player to be recognized as such.

OSU opened the 1985 season with its first night game. The Buckeyes brought in portable lights to play Pittsburgh on Sept. 14. Ohio State beat the Panthers 10-7.

Jim Karsatos completed 12 consecutive passes against Wisconsin in 1985, a single-game OSU record. He is tied with three other players for the record of most consecutive completions (Craig Krenzel, Mike Tomczak, and Bill Mrukowski), but the other players' streaks spanned over two games.

Ohio State was a rare underdog in Ohio Stadium when No. 1 ranked Iowa came to visit in 1985. A tenacious defense, led by Chris Spielman and Pepper Johnson, held the Hawkeyes, led by quarterback Chuck Long, to 13 points. Jim Karsatos passed for 151 yards and George Cooper ran for 104 yards to help the Buckeyes win 22-13.

By The Numbers

Ohio State Buckeyes

FOOTBALL

Michigan scored 86 points against the Buckeyes in 1902, OSU's record for points allowed in a single game. OSU has only allowed 50 points or more three other times: 1946 (Michigan scored 58 points), 1994 (Penn State scored 63 points), and 1890 (Wooster scored 64 points).

Troy Smith set Ohio State's record for total yards gained against Michigan in a single game when he recorded 386 yards (18 rushes for 145 yards and one TD; 13 of 23 passes for 241 yards and two TDs) in 2004. Smith also gained 337 total yards in 2005 and 328 total yards in 2006 while leading the Buckeyes to three consecutive victories against the Wolverines.

In 1986 Cris Carter became OSU's first consensus All-American at the receiver position. He led the team with 1,127 receiving yards and 11 touchdown receptions for the season.

Ohio State has been ranked No. 1 in the AP Poll a total of 86 weeks all-time. The Buckeyes are tied for second with Oklahoma for most weeks ranked No.1, three weeks behind Notre Dame's 89 week total.

The Buckeyes opened the 1986 season with two losses, only the third time in school history this has happened (1892 and 1894). Ohio State bounced back, winning 10 of the next 11 games, including a Cotton Bowl victory over No. 8 Texas A&M.

By The Numbers

Ohio State Buckeyes

FOOTBALL

College football coaching legend Woody Hayes died in his sleep on March 12, 1987. Greater than 10,000 people attended his memorial service, which included a speech given by former President Nixon. Hayes was 74 years old and had been suffering health problems.

In 1987 the Buckeyes beat Michigan 23-20 in Ann Arbor, coach Earl Bruce's last game as OSU head coach. His firing was announced days prior to the game. In support of their coach, players wore white headbands during the game with the inscription "Earl." Ohio State would not beat the Wolverines in Ann Arbor again until 2001, coach Tressel's first season.

Orlando Pace finished fourth in voting for the 1996 Heisman Trophy. He received 87 first place votes and 599 total points. The top-three finishers were Danny Wuerffel, Troy Davis, and Jake Plummer. Pace and John Hicks are the only offensive linemen to have finished in the top four since 1963. Pace made history by becoming the first sophomore to win the Lombardi Award and first two-time winner the following year. As a junior in 1996 he was named Big Ten Offensive Player of the Year and Big Ten MVP. Pace played 13 seasons in the NFL and is a seven time Pro Bowler.

By The Numbers

Ohio State Buckeyes

FOOTBALL

Buckeye fans like to travel. And when Ohio State played Syracuse in 1988, many Buckeye fans filled the Carrier Dome. One way to get the stadium rockin' is for the Ohio State marching band to play "Hang on Sloopy". However, due to the fans' seismic response when the song is played, occupants of the press box felt shaking. Syracuse University officials requested the song not be played again until they had time to test the structural integrity of the press box. The fans and the players rocked to a 26-9 victory.

Ohio State finished 4-6-1 in 1988, the first losing season in 22 years. The Buckeyes were outscored 229-283. A low point was the 7-41 loss to Indiana. This was OSU's second consecutive loss to the Hoosiers, which had not happened since the OSU-Indiana matchups spanning the 1901-03 seasons. The only highpoint of the season was a 36-33 victory over 7th ranked LSU. With only 4:29 remaining, the Buckeyes rallied back from a 13-point deficit. And with just a few seconds remaining, OSU took the lead when Bobby Olive made a diving catch in the end zone.

Featured Figure
The State of Ohio's General Assembly made "Hang on Sloopy" the official rock song of Ohio in 1985, making Ohio the first state to have an official rock song. The first playing of the song by the Ohio State marching band is referenced in the resolution.

By The Numbers

Ohio State Buckeyes

○ ○ ○ • • •

F
O
O
T
B
A
L
L

89

Archie Griffin set OSU's career rushing record with 5,589 yards gained from 1972-75. Eddie George is second with 3,768 yards gained from 1992-95. He averaged 121.5 yards per carry for his career, making him No. 1 on OSU's list for career yards per carry, 27.4 yards higher than No. 2 Jim Otis.

Buckeye halfback Gene Fekete had a non-scoring run of 89 yards against Pittsburgh in 1942, which is Ohio State's record for longest rushing play. The Buckeyes beat the Panthers 59-19, bouncing back from their only loss of the season the previous week against the Wisconsin Badgers. While traveling on a train from Chicago to Madison, several key players became sick after drinking from the train's water fountain and were unable to play in the game. The top ranked Buckeyes lost 7-17 to the 6th ranked Badgers, OSU's only loss of the season.

Featured Figure
Only three Buckeyes have recorded greater than 90 interception yards in a game. Will Allen (San Diego State, 2003) Marlon Kerner (Purdue, 1993), and David Brown (Purdue, 1986) all recorded 100 interception yards in a single game.

By The Numbers

• • • ○ ○ ○

Ohio State Buckeyes

Football

OSU's only loss to a U.S. Service Academy came against Air Force in the 1990 Liberty Bowl. The Buckeye's lost 11-23 to the Falcons. Ohio State was favored by 17 points. In addition, the 6-5 Falcons had given up an average of 24.7 points per game during the season while only scoring an average of 20.8 points per game. The Buckeyes on the other hand averaged 30.7 points per game and only allowed 17.9 points per game prior to the bowl game.

The Buckeyes have surpassed 90 wins in a decade three times: 91 wins in the 1970s and 1990s, and 101 wins in the 2000s.

Ohio State's lowest winning percentage in a decade came in the 1890s when the team finished with a record of 39-40-4 (.494). The Buckeyes ended the decade with a 9-0-1 record, the first in a streak of 13 consecutive winning seasons.

In 1990 natural grass returned as the playing surface at Ohio Stadium. The new turf provided solid ground for Robert Smith. He broke Archie Griffin's freshman rushing record with 1,126 yards. Smith had 177 carries in for a 6.36 yard average. As a freshman in 1972, Archie Griffin gained 867 yards off of 159 carries for an average of 5.45 yards per carry. Smith's freshman rushing record was broken by Maurice Clarett in 2002 when he ran for 1,237 yards off of 222 carries for an average of 5.57 yards per carry.

By The Numbers

Ohio State Buckeyes

FOOTBALL

The Buckeyes' all-time record at Ohio Stadium is 391-107-20, a .774 winning percentage.

In 1991 Carlos Snow led the Buckeyes in rushing yards with 828 yards. He also led the team in 1988 and 1989. He is the only Buckeye to lead the team in rushing yards for more than two seasons since Archie Griffin. However, Griffin remains the only player to lead the team in rushing for four consecutive years (1972-75).

David Boston had 191 catches during his career, averaging 5.2 yards per catch, the highest of any Buckeye. Only eight other players have averaged three or more yards per reception in their career: Joey Galloway (3.0), Gary Williams (3.2), Robert Rein (3.2), Michael Jenkins (3.2), Ted Ginn, Jr. (3.6), Santonio Holmes (3.9), Billy Anders (4.0), and Cris Carter (4.5).

The longest rushing play ever allowed by the Buckeyes was for 91 yards. Iowa's Larry Ferguson set this record in 1960. Only four other players have had rushes of 80 yards or more against OSU: O.J. Simpson (Southern Cal, 80 yards, 1969 Rose Bowl), Clinton Jones (Michigan State, 80 yards, 1965), Daniel DuFrene (Illinois, 80 yards, 2007), and Levi Jackson (Michigan State, 88 yards, 1974).

By The Numbers

Ohio State Buckeyes

○○○•••

FOOTBALL

The Buckeyes finished 5-3 in 1892, their first-ever winning season. Two of the three losses came against Oberlin. The Yeomen outscored the Buckeyes 90-4 in those two matchups.

Richard Ellis became Ohio State's first two-time team captain in 1892. OSU wouldn't have another two-time captain until Archie Griffin in 1975. Since Griffin, five other players have been two-time team captain: Glenn Cobb in 1981-82, Pepper Johnson in 1984-85, Joe Cooper in 2000-01, Steve Bellisari in 2000-01, and James Laurinaitis in 2007-08. Other notable captains are former Michigan head coach Gary Moeller who was team captain in 1962 and Austin Spitler who never started a game prior to being named team captain in 2009. Spitler lived up to the position, playing a key role in helping the Buckeyes win the 2010 Rose Bowl. There have only been three father-son combos: James Herbstreit (1960) and Kirk Herbstreit (1992), Jim Davidson (1964) and Jeff Davidson (1989), and Pepper Johnson (1984-85) and Dionte Johnson (2007).

OSU linebacker Randy Gradishar was inducted into the CoSIDA Academic Hall of Fame in 1992. He is the only athlete from Ohio State to have received this honor.

Featured Figure
Ohio State has the best all-time Big Ten winning percentage among conference teams. OSU is 454-165-24 all-time in Big Ten play for a .725 winning percentage.

By The Numbers

•••○○○

Ohio State Buckeyes

FOOTBALL

By The Numbers

Joey Galloway led the Buckeyes in scoring with 78 points in 1993, the last time a receiver accomplished this feat.

The last time the Buckeyes were shut out was against Michigan in 1993. Ohio State lost 0-28 to the Wolverines.

John Cooper led Ohio State to 10-wins in 1993, his first of five seasons with 10+ wins. During the season the Buckeyes rose in the polls to a No. 3 ranking. They took that ranking into the first-ever Big Ten matchup against Penn State on Oct. 30, 1993, at Ohio Stadium. In addition to welcoming the Nittany Lions into the conference, OSU was looking for its first conference title since 1984. Raymont Harris led the Buckeyes with 151 yards rushing, helping lead the Buckeyes to a 24-6 victory over PSU. The Buckeyes traveled to Wisconsin the following week. The winner would gain control of the Big Ten. Ohio State struggled in the sub-20 degree weather. The Buckeyes drove 99 yards to tie the game 14-14 with 46 seconds left to play. On the ensuing drive, the Badgers moved the ball to OSU's 15-yard line for a last second field goal attempt. Marlon Kerner came off the end to block the field goal and secure a tie. Even though the game ended in a tie, the Buckeyes could have won the Big Ten outright with a win against Michigan. But the Buckeyes would lose 0-28 to a four-loss Wolverine team. With the loss, OSU and Wisconsin tied as Big Ten Champions. Since the Badgers last went to the Rose Bowl in 1963, they got the bid to represent the conference against UCLA.

Ohio State Buckeyes

FOOTBALL

Jim Tressel has led the Buckeyes to a record of 94-21 (.817) since 2001, the second best all-time winning percentage among OSU head coaches.

Since the 1994 game against Michigan, every former OSU football player has been welcomed to form a "Tunnel of Pride" at home games against the Wolverines. Ohio State is 6-2 against the Wolverines since the first "Tunnel of Pride" was formed. One was also formed before the Buckeyes took the field to play Notre Dame in 1995, a 45-26 OSU victory.

In 2009 Terrelle Pryor became the most recent OSU quarterback to pass for 2,000 yards in a season. He is the 16th quarterback to accomplish this feat. Pryor joined the group by completing 167 of 295 attempts for 2,094 yards.

OSU played two games at the Ohio State Fair in 1894. The Buckeyes lost both matchups, 6-12 against Akron and 0-6 against Wittenberg. The games were intended to increase support for the football program.

Featured Figure

Archie Griffin (1976), John Frank (1984), and Craig Krenzel (2004) are the only Buckeyes to have won the NCAA's Top VIII Award given to the nation's top collegiate student athletes. The award was known as the Top V when awarded to Griffin and Frank.

By The Numbers

Ohio State Buckeyes

FOOTBALL

OSU played its first out-of-state road game against the University of Kentucky on Nov. 15, 1895. The Buckeyes beat the Wildcats 8-6.

In 1995, Eddie George led the nation in scoring with 152 points (24 rushing touchdowns, one receiving touchdown, and one two-point conversion).

OSU players received six major college football awards in 1995: Eddie George - Doak Walker, Heisman, Walter Camp, and Maxwell; Terry Glenn - Biletnikoff; and Orlando Pace – Outland. This is the most major college football awards given to Buckeye players in one season. The four major awards won by George also set the mark for most won by an OSU player in a single season.

Ohio State scored 475 points in 1995, an OSU record. The Buckeyes won their first 11 games by an average of 24 points. The closest OSU came to a loss in the first 11 games was a 28-25 victory against Penn State. Eddie George scored the go-ahead touchdown with 1:42 remaining. The Buckeyes closed out the regular season with a loss to the Wolverines. Michigan running back Tim Biakabutuka rushed for 313 yards against OSU, the most ever allowed by a single player in a game in Ohio State history. The Buckeyes followed up the Michigan loss with a 14-20 loss to Tennessee in a sloppy Citrus Bowl. After rising to as high as No.2 in the AP Poll, the Buckeyes finished No. 6 in the final poll after the two consecutive losses.

By The Numbers

Ohio State Buckeyes

FOOTBALL

Andy Katzenmoyer is the only linebacker to lead the Buckeyes in sacks for a single season. "The Big Kat" led the team with 12 sacks for -74 yards in 1996, his freshman year.

In 1896 Ohio State faced Ohio Medical University three times. The Buckeyes held OMU scoreless in all three meetings, beating them 24-0 to open the season, a 0-0 tie, and a 12-0 win. The 2-0-1 record against OMU helped the Buckeyes finish the season 5-5-1. The teams played a total of eight times from 1896 to 1906. OSU's all-time record against Ohio Medical is 5-2-1. OMU merged with Starling Ohio Medical College in 1907 and the newly formed college was acquired by The Ohio State University in 1914.

The 1996 season started with two games in which the Buckeyes scored 70 or more points. OSU scored 450+ points for the second straight season, the only time this has been accomplished in school history. The only slip up of the season was a 9-13 loss to Michigan. With a 9-0 lead in the third quarter, consensus All-American Shawn Springs slipped on a passing play, which allowed Michigan receiver Tai Streets to get the Wolverines on the board with its first touchdown. Michigan added two field goals and shut out the Buckeyes in the second half.

In 1996 Stanley Jackson finished the season with 1,298 passing yards. Not far behind was Joe Germaine with 1,193 passing yards. This is the only time two Buckeyes have recorded 1,000+ passing yards in the same season.

By The Numbers

Ohio State Buckeyes

F
O
O
T
B
A
L
L

The first meeting between Ohio State and Michigan took place at Michigan on Oct. 16, 1897. The Buckeyes lost the game 0-34.

David Boston set OSU's single-game receiving record with 14 receptions against Penn State in 1997. He is also number two on the list with 13 receptions against Indiana in 1996.

The Buckeye defense allowed 297 points in 1989, the record for most allowed in a season. OSU finished the season 8-4 and allowed five opponents to score greater than 30 points.

Ohio State's only win in 1897 came by forfeit. In protest of an OSU touchdown, Ohio Medical left the field. Even though the Buckeyes still trailed by a touchdown after the controversial score, they were awarded a 6-0 victory by forfeit. OSU finished the season 1-7-1.

OSU recorded its 700th all-time victory against Illinois on Nov. 15, 1997.

Featured Figure
Santonio Holmes is the only Buckeye to be named Super Bowl MVP. He was named MVP after gaining 131 yards on nine receptions and catching the go-ahead touchdown for the Pittsburgh Steelers against the Arizona Cardinals in Super Bowl XLIII.

By The Numbers

Ohio State Buckeyes

FOOTBALL

Joe Germaine set Ohio State's single-season record for passing yards in 1998 with 3,330 yards and 25 touchdowns. Bobby Hoying is the only other OSU quarterback to surpass 3,000 yards in a season. He recorded 3,269 yards in 1995 with 29 touchdown passes. Other single-season records set by Germaine in 1998 include: pass attempts (384), pass completions (230), passing yards per game (277.5), 200-yard passing games (11), and 300-yard passing games (7). His accomplishments for the season earned him the Chicago Tribune's Silver Football Award as the Big Ten's MVP.

The Buckeyes called Ohio Field home from 1898 to 1921 before moving to Ohio Stadium in 1922. The original capacity of Ohio Field was around 5,000. Even though capacity grew, it became too small for the growing Buckeye fan base.

Rob Murphy was named consensus All-American in 1998, the most recent OSU offensive lineman to be named as such. This was his second consecutive year as consensus All-American.

The most passes completed in a game by Ohio State are 34, accomplished against Indiana in 1998. Only two other times has OSU completed 30 or more passes in a game (32 against Penn State in 1997 and 31 against Florida State in 1981).

By The Numbers

Ohio State Buckeyes

FOOTBALL

99

Bill Willis' jersey number 99 was retired by OSU on Nov. 3, 2007. From 1942-44, Willis started for the Buckeyes on both the offensive and defensive lines. He became OSU's first black All-American in 1943. He is a member of both the College Football and Pro Football Halls of Fame and is considered to be the first black player to start in professional football.

The Buckeyes went 9-0-1 in 1899, their first-ever undefeated season. The only points the Buckeyes allowed all season were in a 5-5 tie against Case, a Buckeye single-season record for fewest points allowed in a season. OSU beat Oberlin for the first time in seven meetings, being outscored by 190 points in the previous matchups. A returned fumble led to the only points of the game as Ohio State won 6-0.

The last time the Buckeyes had a losing record in the Big Ten was in 1999. OSU finished 3-5 in conference play, tied for eighth place.

John Cooper recorded his 100th victory as an OSU head coach on Sept. 25, 1999. The Buckeyes beat the Cincinnati Bearcats 34-20.

The Buckeyes recorded 19 tackles for loss against Penn State in 1999, an OSU single-game record. Even so, the No. 18 ranked Buckeyes lost 10-23 to the No.2 ranked Nittany Lions.

By The Numbers

Ohio State Buckeyes

○ ○ ○ • • •

F
O
O
O
Only two Buckeyes have recorded 100 or more solo tackles in a single season: Chris Spielman recorded 105 solo tackles in 1986 and Tom Cousineau 102 solo tackles in 1976 and 142 solo tackles in 1978.

T
B
Ohio State has averaged over 100,000 in attendance since 2001.

A
L
L
OSU had three players rush for 100 or more yards in the same game on three separate occasions. The last time was in 1989 when Dante Lee (157), Scottie Graham (102) and Carlos Snow (100) combined for 359 rushing yards against Northwestern.

Two Buckeyes have recorded 100+ yards receiving in the same game on 14 occasions. Most recently in 2005 when Ted Ginn, Jr. and Santonio Holmes gained 167 and 124 yards respectively against Notre Dame.

David Boston holds the OSU record for most 100+ yard receiving games in a career with 14. He recorded nine 100+ yard receiving games in 1998, which is OSU's single-season record.

Ohio State recorded its 100th victory against Vanderbilt on Nov. 14, 1908. OSU's all-time record following the game stood at 100-62-12.

By The Numbers

• • • ○ ○ ○

All information in this book is valid as of the end of the 2009 season.